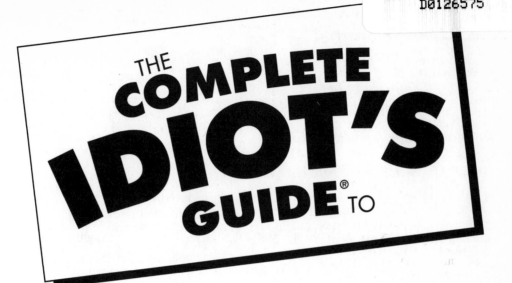

THE COMPLETE IDIOT'S GUIDE® TO

Enhancing Self-Esteem

by Mark J. Warner

ALPHA

A member of Penguin Group (USA) Inc.

This book is dedicated to:

God, my heavenly father

David, my earthly father

Rosanna, my angel mother

Jennie, my soulmate

Sarah and Katie, my life treasures

International Standard Book Number: 0-02862930-2
Library of Congress Catalog Card Number: Information available on request.

07 06 05   10 9

Interpretation of the printing code: the rightmost number of the first series of numbers is the year of the book's printing; the rightmost number of the second series of numbers is the number of the book's printing. For example, a printing code of 99-1 shows that the first printing occurred in 1999.

Printed in the United States of America

Note: This publication contains the opinions and ideas of its author. It is intended to provide helpful and informative material on the subject matter covered. It is sold with the understanding that the author and publisher are not engaged in rendering professional services in the book. If the reader requires personal assistance or advice, a competent professional should be consulted.

The author and publisher specifically disclaim any responsibility for any liability, loss or risk, personal or otherwise, which is incurred as a consequence, directly or indirectly, of the use and application of any of the contents of this book.

Alpha Development Team

Publisher
Kathy Nebenhaus

Editorial Director
Gary M. Krebs

Managing Editor
Bob Shuman

Marketing Brand Manager
Felice Primeau

Editor
Jessica Faust

Development Editors
Phil Kitchel
Amy Zavatto

Production Team

Production Editor
Suzanne Snyder

Copy Editor
Gail Burlakoff

Cover Designer
Mike Freeland

Photo Editor
Richard H. Fox

Illustrator
Jody P. Schaeffer

Designer
Nathan Clement

Indexer
Lisa Stumpf

Layout/Proofreading
Angela Calvert
Mary Hunt

Contents at a Glance

Contents

Foreword

If right now you're strolling through the Self-Help section of the bookstore, you can see how many self-esteem books there are on the shelves. Why on earth are we so interested in these books? What are we looking for when we first crack the cover of a new title and start thumbing through its pages?

We want the words to be familiar and ring true to our experience. Otherwise the advice will just sit on the page: we'll distrust it and so we'll never apply it to our lives. But we also want to discover something new, something that speaks to us in a way we haven't quite managed to speak to ourselves. Like a good friend, a good book is always familiar to us, yet always manages to surprise us. It says just the right thing in just the right way, telling us what we already—in some way—know, but always need to rediscover.

The book you're now reading is one of these good books. There is no ego on its pages, no hidden agenda, and no attempt to promise us everything we ever wanted in exchange for our life savings. When you were little, did you ever read Dr. Seuss's *My Book about Me*? It's the kind of book that, whenever you run across it on your book-shelf, you remember how it felt as a five-year-old to work through it, answer its questions, and discover more about yourself. It's not just a part of your history, it's part of your identity. Well, Mark Warner's book is *My Book about Me* for grown-ups who are not afraid to be children again. Instead of shoe sizes and favorite colors, it starts us thinking about favorite memories, goals, and habits. But it's written with as much sheer joy as the Dr. Seuss book, and it's as fun to read as well!

If you've purchased self-esteem books before, or if you watch enough info-mercials, you know that some writers stand (or think they stand) on the mountaintop, shouting their platitudes down to those on the paths below. Mark Warner isn't standing on the mountaintop: he's standing right next to us. If, in spite of our fears, we hear the author's voice and risk the walk, it's because we know he's walking the path with us.

I'll give away one of the book's secrets right up front: this path is a winding one. Are you looking for a book to give you all the answers? Then put this book down *immediately!* It will inspire you to rethink your priorities, examine your relationships, and even doubt that you are who you say you are. In short, things will get a little unpredictable. But that's the whole spirit behind Mark Warner's words. Sometimes we discover new information and gain assurance. Other times, though, what we think we are sure of turns out to be an illusion, and we have to start thinking all over again. This is the key to self-esteem: to break free of our boundaries and to start exploring. The exploration itself gives us our identity and connects us to others.

In this book and its author, you have discovered a travel companion and a friend worthy of your trust. So grab your backpack, and let the adventure begin.

Dr. John N. Jones

Dr. Jones, who was trained in world religions (Harvard Divinity School) and philosophy of religion (Yale University), is a widely-published authority on spirituality.

Introduction

Welcome! I'm pleased that we get to share part of life's journey together. Since we can't travel face-to-face, we get to do it the next best way—through the pages of a book.

Honest Abe, Maslow that is, brought a lot of notoriety to the term *self-esteem*. He was the daddy of humanistic psychology and proposed a hierarchy of needs that is now featured in every introductory psychology text known to humankind. Self-esteem is nestled inside the hierarchy and is an essential ingredient needed to reach the pinnacle called self-actualization. Maslow basically defined self-esteem as self-respect, how you feel about yourself.

The framework for the book is simple yet provocative. The book is divided into eight parts, each representing a component of the acronym I RESPECT. The framework serves a twofold purpose: (1) to provide the glue which holds the chapters together, and (2) to offer life components that can be made operational to promote positive change. I use the I RESPECT acronym because respect for self and others is the basis for positive self-esteem and optimal living. The acronym components follow:

I = Integrity: The Essence of You

R = Risk Taking: Become a Change Hugger

E = Emotions: Experiencin' and Expressin'

S = Service: Help Others and Help Thyself

P = Perspective: Get It!

E = Exercise Decision Making: Exercise Without the Sweat

C = Communication: Stop, Look, Listen, Grow!

T = Teamwork: The Power of One Plus

This book differs from others in that it provides a holistic view of life. Our daily adventures affect all aspects of our lives and all aspects of our lives affect our daily adventures. Reciprocity at its finest. The challenge for us is to find the balance—the optimal relationship between the competing forces in our lives.

This book is also different from others in that it takes a nonthreatening, humorous, user-friendly approach to a complex subject—*you*. It provides material that effectively balances the challenge and support necessary for personal growth. Overall, the individual topics in the book are woven together with a common thread: care. The compound effect of all of these elements is personal change.

Throughout my life I have collected stories, quotes, and insights. I've written them on napkins, post-its, business cards, and paper scraps—with the purpose of sharing the information with others. The wisdom in this book comes from many sources: books, mentors, parents, friends, teachers, and life. I apologize to the original authors of those thoughts and ideas that I can't properly reference. The purpose of this book is growth. We live life more fully through the collective wisdom of our experiences.

Let's start the journey.

In Addition...

You will probably want to take advantage of the little nuggets of reflection distributed throughout the text. They will give you pieces of insight and help add perspective to the topics being discussed.

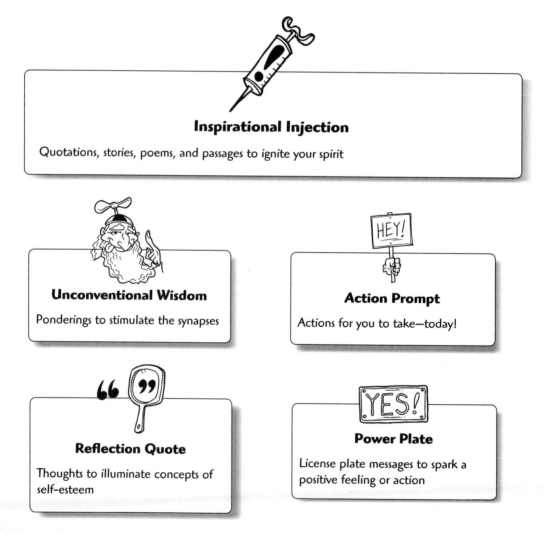

Inspirational Injection

Quotations, stories, poems, and passages to ignite your spirit

Unconventional Wisdom

Ponderings to stimulate the synapses

Action Prompt

Actions for you to take—today!

Reflection Quote

Thoughts to illuminate concepts of self-esteem

Power Plate

License plate messages to spark a positive feeling or action

Acknowledgments

This book came to fruition because of the collaborative efforts of many. Without their help it would only be a rough draft inside my computer.

My thanks to:

Jennie, my wife, who has always encouraged me to follow my dreams and provided the support that has helped me reach them.

Trent Price, my agent, whose persistence and expertise made this book a reality.

Sarah Matthes and Randy Mitchell, who graciously read the initial manuscript and provided keen insights and comments. The final product is much better because of the care and time they invested.

John Jones, development editor, who made this process smooth and enjoyable. His guidance, reflection, support, and demeanor enriched the experience. His work went beyond that of a development editor to the roles of teacher, inquisitor, and colleague.

Suzanne Snyder, production editor, for her expert detail management and expeditiously moving the manuscript through the process; Gail Burlakoff, copy editor, whose insights and careful work enhanced the clarity of the book; and Nancy Mikhail, then acquisitions editor at Alpha Books, who was my first introduction to Alpha Books and graciously welcomed me there. All the folks personified a "collaborative spirit," and as a result of their efforts the process was rewarding and fulfilling. My thanks to them for making the book better than the one they received.

Thanks to the following people for granting permission to use works previously published:

Ken Sheldon, editor, for allowing me to use excerpts and adaptations of my articles originally published in *Executive Excellence* and *Personal Excellence*: "Enhancing Self-Esteem," "Executive Vulnerability," "Life Transitions," "Why Teams Fail—How Teams Succeed," "In Search of Souls," and "Life Cards."

Mark L. Usry, who co-authored "Executive Vulnerability."

Jack H. Presbury, for his wonderful poem, "Icarus."

Feel Free to Contact Me!

If you would like to respond to the thoughts in this book, share your own thoughts, or if you wish to contact me about my work as a speaker, consultant, and teacher, please contact me at the following address. I'd love to hear from you!

Mark J. Warner
Alumnae 208 MSC 7608
James Madison University
Harrisonburg, VA 22807

I respect

Part 1
Integrity:
The Essence of YOU

Each time you are honest and conduct yourself with honesty, a success force will drive you toward greater success. Each time you lie, even with a little white lie, there are strong forces pushing you toward failure.

Joseph Sugarman

It is easy for you to get caught up in your image—how you and others see you from the outside. In this part of the book, you'll begin to look beneath the exterior image to the person inside. As you do so, you'll discover ways that you are unique—labels that you or others give you just can't do justice to who you really are. You might also discover an unattractive gap between what you say about your actions and thoughts and your real actions and thoughts. Restoring your integrity will mean bringing into line what you promise and what you deliver.

Who Is That in the Mirror?

"Mirror mirror on the wall, who's the fairest one of all?"

That line from *Snow White* nudges some childhood memories, doesn't it? It also raises an interesting question.

People have been dialoguing with mirrors throughout history. It goes all the way back to caveperson Og. One day Og was peering over a calm body of water and, happening to look down, he saw someone staring back. Og quickly retreated, startled at the image he saw. Then he crept back to the water's edge and cautiously peeked at the water. This time he found himself staring at the image. He smiled at it, and it smiled back. He frowned at it, it frowned back. He made a funny face at it, it made a funny face back. After a little reflection (sorry, I couldn't resist) he scratched his head and said, "Who is that? Is that me?...Boy, I need a haircut!" The first mirror was discovered.

Twas the Day of the Test

'Twas the day of the test,
and life was the class.
It started routinely
staring at your mirror glass.

Test questions would greet you
from morning 'til night
and your search would be inward

to do what was right.
First was the question from your son (he turned 13 two days ago)
who asked "today, can I be 12
to pay less at the picture show?"

And then there was the store trip
with the cashier in distraction
who gave you back 10 dollars more
than due from the transaction.

Oh yes[md]and those income taxes

that were bleeding your resources dry. Should you fudge the numbers just a bit?
(So what's a little white lie?)

These questions and more all tried you and tested your sense of soul.
But the thoughtful responses you offered supported your integrity goals.

Your behavior matched your words, all right, and you acted with such class
that peace enveloped you that night
as you winked at the mirror glass.

Mark Warner

Don't Cheat the Person in the Glass

Remember Narcissus? In Greek mythology, he was a person of great beauty who fell in love with his own reflection in a pool of water. Whenever he went to touch the image, to kiss it, to hug it…it became distorted and broken. Because he was not able to grasp the image he loved, he died of grief. He lost his life because he was focused on an external image, not on internal substance.

Even though Narcissus looked at the person in the glass, he cheated him. It's easy for you, too, to cheat that person when you look only at the visual reflection staring back, the same image that a stranger sees. For a truer assessment, however, you need to look beyond the surface presence and steal inward. Gaze beyond the freckles, the lines, the hair—go deeper. Who really *is* that person looking back?

Sometimes we try to mask the interior of our personhood by decorating the exterior with design and style. We think that if we focus on the physical aspects of our being, then we won't have to confront the essence. *Wrong!*

You can't hide yourself from yourself. Nor do you want to. Integration of the different aspects of yourself enables you to become more whole.

Unconventional Wisdom

To be who you really are is the easiest and hardest thing you will ever do.

Smoke and Mirrors

The great illusionists pull rabbits from hats, thrust swords through people without drawing blood, and even make elephants disappear. Ahh, smoke and mirrors—some even call it magic. The illusions you see on the stage and screen are intended for fun, to entertain. When we use smoke and mirrors to define ourselves, however, the fun stops and damage begins. Sometimes your subconscious fabricates images that are not consistent with your true self, masking the inconsistencies and hiding behind the guise of self-protection. But is it really self-protection? Often the answer is "no." Self-protection of this variety is merely a method of surrender, keeping you from experiencing the true essence of your humanness. While surrender impedes growth, feeling and being fosters personal growth. When you peel away the layers of self-deception, an authentic treasure is revealed—*you*.

It is important to note that your personal smoke-and-mirrors routine can be a result of both conscious and subconscious processes. When consciously employed, the only person on whom the trick is played is you.

Reflection Quote

The measure of an individual's real character is what that person does when he or she knows that no one else will find out.

—MacSalay

You weave the threads of weaknesses and strengths to create a tapestry of life. It takes all aspects of you, even the warts, to be integrated and whole. But when you acknowledge and learn from the many aspects of yourself, you create a genuine sense of self.

The Image—Is Right Right or Right Left?

Take a peek in the mirror. The image staring back seems to be an accurate reflection of you. But wait a minute. Look again. Imagine that you have a brush in your hand. The person in the glass is holding the brush in the opposite hand. So the image is inaccurate.

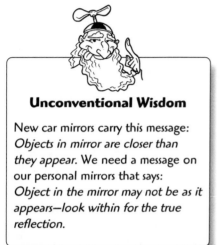

Unconventional Wisdom

New car mirrors carry this message: *Objects in mirror are closer than they appear.* We need a message on our personal mirrors that says: *Object in the mirror may not be as it appears—look within for the true reflection.*

You don't look in the mirror and consciously say to yourself, "That image is inaccurate!" At some point, however, you did acknowledge that fact. You intellectually knew the image was not what it appeared to be, but you came to accept and ignore the inaccuracy.

Hmm. Do you ever do that in life? My guess is that you unconsciously accept, all the time, things that are not accurate. Go back to the smoke and mirrors. Our conscious and subconscious minds play tricks on us all the time. So how do you see through these illusions to get an accurate and realistic perception of yourself?

Here are some questions for you to consider. Before you answer any, take an objective step back. Look at yourself with different eyes. Try to release the hold that your subjective self has on you so that you can start learning to see yourself from the outside.

1. Some of my major accomplishments in life are:

   _____

   _____

2. A time I really felt good about myself was when:

   _____

   _____

3. One of my favorite compliments was:

   _____

   _____

4. My strongest gifts are:

   _____

   _____

Now for some futurist statements. Remember, *you* create your future.

1. I want people to say that I am:

   _____

   _____

2. One thing I want to accomplish in my life is:

   _____

   _____

3. I can touch someone else's life by:

   _____

   _____

4. I will treat the person in the mirror differently and affirm myself with these words:

   _____

   _____

The challenge is to address the true issues and feelings and not let them get clouded and distorted through self-imposed smoke and mirrors. Take the challenge.

Am I Who I Am?

Read this title backwards—really fast. Did it read as you thought it would? It was identical to the way you read it the first time. Your high school English teacher will tell you that it is a palindrome, in this instance, a palindromic phrase—it reads the same forward as backward.

Back to the question. Am I Who I Am? I hope you are who you are, but the best way to find out is to ask yourself some questions. The questions are easy; the answers might be a little more difficult.

➤ Do I keep my promises?

➤ Do my behaviors match my beliefs?

➤ Do I "walk my talk"?

➤ Am I who I say I am?

Integrity—The Quick Check

Kouzes and Posner, two leadership gurus, have come up with a quick integrity check. It's this simple:

DWWSWWD

OK. Let's see whether you learned anything. English enthusiasts call this a what? Yes, another palindrome. (The bonus with this book is that you get to learn about more than just life.) The actual phrase that these letters represent is not quite as palindramatic, but it's a great phrase anyway:

Do What We Say We Will Do

Kouzes and Posner hit the mark! Such an easy statement, but packed with great power.

Now gauge yourself against the statement. Do you do what you say you do? Is your answer as easy as the question? You are the only one on this earth who can give the true answer.

Power Plate

KPPRMSS

Get in Touch with the "Big V"

Have you ever participated in a values clarification activity? Sometimes our initial response is, "I really don't want to do this." But after we drag ourselves through the activity, our tone changes and we say, "Wow, I didn't know that about myself."

Reflection Quote

The future belongs to those who believe in the beauty of their dreams.

—Eleanor Roosevelt

The maxim that the more you know about yourself, the more effectively you can gauge and enhance your integrity, is so true. Listen to the clarion call, "Know Thyself."

Ask yourself these questions to get started:

1. Who am I?

_____

_____

2. What do I believe?

_____

_____

3. What is important to me?

_____

_____

4. What is my purpose in life?

_____

_____

Usually we don't ask these value questions until we're confronted with a situation that prompts us to have to answer them. This is your chance to be proactive. Start that clarification today—avoid the rush.

Inspirational Injection

Have you ever stepped onto an elevator and felt a sense of discomfort as the doors closed and you were confined with a set of strangers? Remember the awkward silence that permeated the den-like cubicle? Eyes stared straight ahead or strained downward. This scene is all too familiar.

Here's the solution. All elevators should be required to have, attached to the inside of the doors, carnival-type mirrors that distort appearances. When the doors shut, the laughter begins. Folks loosen up and a slice of life has just been served.

Dealing with Distorted Mirrors

Have you ever been to a carnival and visited a "house of mirrors"? You walk by one mirror and you are as thin as a spaghetti noodle. You walk by another mirror and your body resembles an avocado. Yet another one makes you look like a person made from coiled pipe cleaners. Distortion at its finest.

Without being aware of it, do you carry around a carnival mirror in your pocket, grasping it when you consider who you are? Do you ever hear yourself saying things like the following?

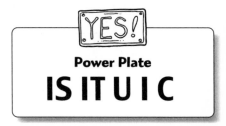

Power Plate

IS IT U I C

➤ This little white lie won't hurt anyone.

➤ I'll call in sick to work today; it's too pretty a day to spend sitting in my office.

➤ Nobody will miss this $5.

➤ I told my client I would come see him today but I don't feel like it. Maybe tomorrow.

Sometimes you might yield to these notions to deal with life in the short term. The challenge is to make decisions for the long term. Integrity is not bound by time. Integrity *is*.

Reflection Quote

If I have lost every friend on earth, I shall at least have one friend left, and that friend shall be down inside of me.

—Unknown

Loving the Person in the Mirror

Have a love affair…with yourself. I'm not talking about an egocentric extravaganza of self-adulation. Rather, I'm talking about a loving sense of self grounded in personal acceptance—warts and all.

Granted that there are some days when it is easier to love yourself than others, your challenge is to increase the number of days. You might be thinking, "How do I do that?" Great question. Let's do what we are always taught not to do—answer a question with some questions.

1. What are two positive things related to my job/school?

_____

_____

2. What are two positive aspects of my home life?

_____

_____

3. What are two positive aspects of my fitness and health?

_____

_____

4. What are two positive aspects of my spiritual life?

_____

_____

If you get to this point and have no answers and a lot of frustration, I challenge you to think a little harder. The answers are there. Don't bury the positive or give higher authority to the negative in your life. *You* decide what to focus on, so go for the good aspects of yourself.

If you skipped over the questions before, go back and give them another shot.

Mirror Messages

How many times a day do you look in a mirror? Everyone looks in a mirror at least once a day. Some look 50 times a day. Where are you on this continuum?

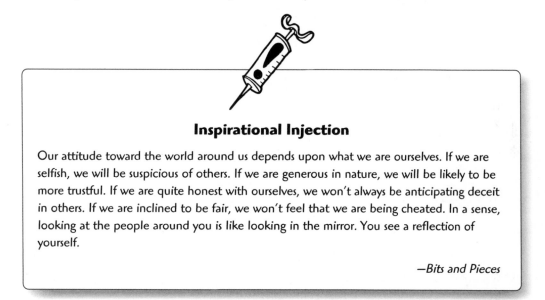

Inspirational Injection

Our attitude toward the world around us depends upon what we are ourselves. If we are selfish, we will be suspicious of others. If we are generous in nature, we will be likely to be more trustful. If we are quite honest with ourselves, we won't always be anticipating deceit in others. If we are inclined to be fair, we won't feel that we are being cheated. In a sense, looking at the people around you is like looking in the mirror. You see a reflection of yourself.

—Bits and Pieces

Mirror-looking is equivalent to message-sending. You talk to yourself when you look in a mirror. You may utter phrases like these:

➤ You look great today.

➤ You look awful today.

➤ You look fat today.

➤ You look skinny today.

➤ You have more gray hair today.

➤ You have less hair than yesterday.

Often your responses gravitate toward the negative side of the continuum. Move yourself to the positive side. Self-help folks have known for years that repeated thoughts create repeated feelings and actions. You are in control of your thoughts and actions. Make them work *for* you instead of *against* you.

When you look in the mirror, remember that you have some incredible gifts and talents. You have the opportunity to make a difference in this world. But you must take charge. Create your own life!

Entertain Introspective Revelations

We grow through introspection and the revelations that surface in our lives. These help us enhance our integrity and sense of self. I'll share one of my revelations with you.

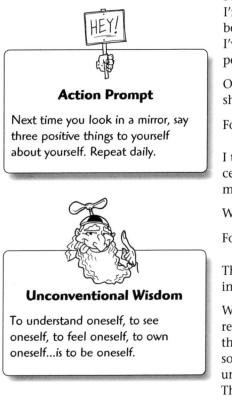

Action Prompt

Next time you look in a mirror, say three positive things to yourself about yourself. Repeat daily.

Unconventional Wisdom

To understand oneself, to see oneself, to feel oneself, to own oneself...is to be oneself.

I have to confess—I'm going bald. I must tell you that I'm not excited about the prospect, but I feel better now because I discovered why this is happening to me. Yes—I've had a revelation that's helped me to put things in perspective.

One morning I was taking a shower. I picked up my shampoo bottle and read the label:

For *fine hair* and *more body*

I thought to myself, "My hair is fine enough and I certainly don't want more body." (My waistline reminds me of that.)

What I want is a shampoo that says:

For *more hair* and a *fine body*

This is the kind of shampoo I'm in the market for. If you invent this kind, please let me know!

When you think about what really makes up *you,* what is really important, it's not your hairline, the size of your thighs, or your height. Rather, it is your heart, mind, and soul. It is the inside. It is this part of you that allows your uniqueness, your greatest treasure, to show through. That is the greatest gift—and you already have it.

The Least You Need to Know

➤ You are the fairest of them all.

➤ Live so that you love the reflection.

➤ Discard distorting carnival mirrors, unless they're used only for fun.

➤ Acknowledge and appreciate your positive attributes.

Chapter 2

Be *YOU*-nique

Fashion style, word style, walk style, hair style, play style, car style, work style, house style, keep-up-with-the-Joneses style…whatever happened to *your* style? Yes, your individualized, idiosyncratic, unique, one-of-a-kind style. *You.*

Do you ever feel as though you get caught up conforming to your friends, to ads, to cocktail party talk? It happens to all of us. Well, today is a special day. Today you can take the challenge to *own* yourself—to be uniquely you. You may have to do a little searching first, but you will like what you find. The discovery will be you, the genuine you, the authentic you, the real you—the you others deserve and will be privileged to see.

Imprints and What Makes You You-nique

We leave behind us several kinds of imprints, but they are actually very different.

➤ **Fingerprints** are undeniable evidence of who you are. You leave them on eye-glasses, you leave them on furniture, you leave them on your car, you leave them any time you touch hard smooth objects with your bare hands. The swirly lines on the tips of your fingers provide the maps of your individuality.

➤ **Footprints** show where you have been, show what direction you were headed, and show whether you were wearing shoes—sometimes. They don't show in the sand washed by a wave, on the concrete sidewalk, or on the rock you are climbing.

➤ **Voiceprints** can be captured on tape, but they are not as reliable as we like to think. Your baby recognizes your voice, your best friend recognizes your voice. But what happens when you have a cold? Your voice is disguised, masked as the voice of another. Although unique, voiceprints are much harder to detect than fingerprints or footprints.

Inspirational Injection

Footprints in the Sand

One night a man had a dream.

He dreamed he was walking along the beach with God.

Across the sky flashed scenes from his life.

For each scene, he noticed two sets of footprints in the sand; one belonging to him, and the other to God.

When the last scene of his life flashed before him, he looked back at the footprints in the sand.

He noticed that many times along the path of his life there was only one set of footprints.

He also noticed that it happened at the very lowest and saddest times in his life.

This really bothered him and he questioned God about it.

"God, you said that once I decided to follow you, you'd walk with me all the way.

But I have noticed that during the most troublesome times in my life there is only one set of footprints.

I don't understand why when I needed you most you would leave me."

God replied, "My precious, precious child, I love you and I would never leave you.

During your times of trial and suffering, when you see only one set of footprints in the sand it was then that I carried you."

—Unknown

All of these prints can be obscured, wiped away, or smudged, but there is another kind of print that is never wiped away—the heart print.

Heartprints

When you combine fingerprints, footprints, and voiceprints, you become a detective's dream. He will feel that he now can identify you. But there is a catch. All these prints, the physical manifestations of who you are, are insignificant compared to the major print of your life—your *heartprint*.

Your heartprint is what you leave when you touch the life of another person. Unlike your fingerprint, with a heartprint there are no lines, there are no sole or toe marks like those on a footprint, and there are no sound-wave peaks like those on a voiceprint. What you see instead is the impact and effect you can have on another's life. You might see a smile in return for a greeting or a tear when sharing an emotion, or feel the warmth of a hug in return for your consoling listening.

Fingerprints, footprints, and voiceprints are all transitory elements of life. Heartprints, however, leave indelible imprints, ones that sustain and enrich a life for years to come.

The only way to leave a true heartprint is to be uniquely you and to share with another person the essence of who you are—no masks, no charades, just the bona fide you.

The magic about sharing the uniquely original you is that the more you do it, the more unique you become. You begin to feel more comfortable and more fulfilled personally. At first this step into Uniqueland might cause you some trepidation, but the journey will be richly rewarded.

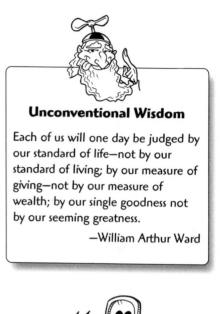

Unconventional Wisdom

Each of us will one day be judged by our standard of life—not by our standard of living; by our measure of giving—not by our measure of wealth; by our single goodness not by our seeming greatness.

—William Arthur Ward

Reflection Quote

If we are to achieve a richer culture, rich in contrasting values, we must recognize the whole gamut of human potentialities, and so weave a less arbitrary social fabric, one in which each diverse human gift will find a fitting place.

—Margaret Mead

You-nique Inventory

Take a minute to reflect upon your uniqueness. Self-discovery comes through self-probing and introspection. Be an introspector!

1. How would my best friend describe me?

   _____

   _____

2. How am I different from anyone else I know?

   _____

   _____

3. What do I do already (and what can I do) to make someone else smile?

   _____

   _____

4. What is one thing I want to do before I die?

   _____

   _____

Oh, by the way, look at question 4 again. What will it take to realize this dream/goal/aspiration? Why are you waiting?

Discover Thyself

So how do we learn who we are? How do we discover the riches within? It is not an easy task. It takes time, patience, and a willingness to grow. Self-discovery comes not only by accident but by intentional pursuit. When you seek to discover yourself, you learn much more than when you passively let life's lessons come to you.

Think about the many life experiences you are exposed to. You certainly don't learn from all of them, but you do learn from those that somehow grab your attention. You can exponentially increase the amount of learning you do just by making the commitment to learn from more experiences.

Reflection Quote

Anyone who sets out on a journey of self-development will be aided. There will be guides and teachers who will appear, and spiritual protectors to watch over the traveler. No test will be given that the traveler does not already have the strength to meet.

—The Sacred Tree

One of the modes of self-discovery is to emulate behaviors we see in others. For example, you might see someone doing something that you like and say to yourself, "Wow, I like what she did. I'm going to try on that behavior and see how it fits." For example, whenever I see a public speaker effectively using a behavioral technique to make a point, I try to remember how she got the point across and adapt her technique to my own speaking.

If you like the way the behavior feels you might make it a part of you. On the other hand, you might try a behavior and say, "Whoa, that's not me." Has that ever happened to you? Bit by bit, piece by piece, you put the puzzle of self together. It is okay and natural to emulate others, but never to the extent that you want to *become* them. Become you and only you.

The Low-Down on Labels

Just look around. Labels are everywhere. Over there you gaze at a guy with the label on the outside of his shirt for all to see. You look at the bottled beverage you are sipping and the label greets you in all its glory. You glance at the TV and see its label front and center. Here a label, there a label, everywhere a label label. Society promotes 'em.

Labeling things is not a problem. When people become the objects of labeling, however, it gets scary. Labels are the enemy of uniqueness. Too often, when someone labels another person, the connotations associated with the label are negative. For example, when someone says, "He is a whale," the reference is not to the prowess of a sea creature adeptly maneuvering through the water or to high intelligence. And then there are those generic jokes that circulate around cocktail parties, office corridors, and computer e-mail —you supply the label of the group of the week to abuse. And remember, even giving someone a "good" label can be limiting to the person and to yourself. It is a sad state of affairs when humans feel that they need to diminish someone else in order to enhance their own sense of self. When we label someone else, however, *two* people are diminished—the labelee and the labeler. Don't be a labeler.

Power Plate

UDSCVRU

Unconventional Wisdom

Label things, not people.

Reflection Quote

My reason for preferring the darkness is that in the dark you have to describe yourself. In the daylight other people describe you.

—Fynn

Label-Understanding Continuum

Picture this continuum. On the far left is the word "Label." On the far right is the word "Understanding."

Label <————————————————————————————> Understanding

The more you know about someone, the closer you approach the understanding point on the continuum, and the less the label that you originally attached to the person fits.

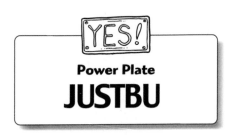

Power Plate

JUSTBU

In fact, have you ever heard yourself say, "My first impression of you was totally different from the way I view you now"? I'll also bet that the first impression had a label attached.

When you make a commitment to understand others, then your labeling of others begins to unravel. In fact, the labels are replaced with respect for the uniqueness of the individual.

Unlabel Thyself

Now comes the hard part. Do you ever label yourself? Do you ever call yourself stupid, a dummy, a fool? Sometimes it is much easier not to label others than not to label ourselves (now that was a mouthful).

Action Prompt

The next time you hear yourself labeling yourself, replace the negative label with a positive affirmation.

When you default to labeling yourself, you do yourself a tremendous disservice. As we know, we become what we repeatedly tell ourselves we are. Don't set yourself a trap.

What are the labels you use for yourself? (Think about your appearance, personality, intelligence, and so forth.)

_____

_____

_____

_____

Not so pretty, are they?

Identify four things you can do to eliminate negative self-labels from your silent or audible vocabulary.

1.   3.

2.   4.

Labels support unhappiness and unfulfilled living. Our job is to create for ourselves a great life. Part of that is determined by how we greet the world. Mark—great segue into the next section!

Smile-itis: Catch It!

She rode in her wheelchair like a queen on a throne. Folks who passed her were immediately attracted to her radiant smile. Years later, when she was totally bed-ridden, visitors were still drawn to her beaming smile. Although a quadriplegic, the one constant of her existence was her quick smile, warming the room and the hearts of all who entered. This woman with the gorgeous smile was my Mom.

Smiles are incredible things. They transcend continental borders, cultures, age, and gender. They are not learned—smiles are instinctual. Smiles can connect you with a total stranger, comfort a sick child, enhance an intimate moment, and warm your soul. What a gift—and it was given to you, *free.*

So if smiles are natural and instinctual, why even discuss them? Because, unfortunately, sometimes our reactions to life's events clog up the smile passages and don't let the message get through. Some little guys inside your head are telling the brain to pull up the corners of your mouth, but some other voices are interrupting these guys with commands of worry and preoccupation.

Unconventional Wisdom

If you smile at me, I will understand, 'cause that is something everybody everywhere does in the same language.

—Stephen Stills

Smile Solutions

You can construct your life so that the smile guys win, but this will take a little conscious effort. Think about what makes you smile most. Is it seeing a child? Is it when you are creating? Is it when you are at peace? Is it when you are scrubbing the floor? Watching a movie? Being your true self?

What are three smile situations for you?

Power Plate

I SMIL 4 U

1. _____

_____

_____

2. _____
_____
_____

3. _____
_____
_____

By identifying when you smile most, you take the first step towards understanding what makes you feel good. When you know what makes you feel good, then, whenever you want to have a smile sensation, you can employ that activity—by doing it or even just remembering it. You are the best monitor for this project.

Smile Beneficiaries

So, who really benefits from smiles? With smiles, the math is interesting. Smiles manifest magic in multiples. Think about what one smile can do. If you are by yourself, it can make you feel good. If you are with one other person, two people now feel good. If you are speaking with a group of people and smile, the group feels good. The multiplication magic is working. Your smile in a group makes the others smile. When the others smile and look at each other, their smiles end up stimulating other smiles. As a friend of mine says as a greeting, "Smiles at you!"

If you are responsible for your own enthusiasm, then you are also responsible for your own smiles. Fortunately, there is a symbiotic relationship between enthusiasm and smiles—one begets the other. Nice arrangement.

Action Prompt

Next time you are feeling a little low, create a smile situation... even if you don't feel like it. The results will be worth the effort.

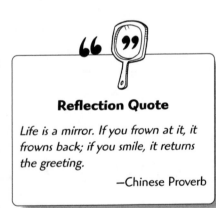

Reflection Quote

Life is a mirror. If you frown at it, it frowns back; if you smile, it returns the greeting.

—Chinese Proverb

Smile Trial

Now is your opportunity to be the judge, but you can't be the judge until you have completed the following test. On a piece of paper (or if you want to be like a famous author, use a napkin), make four columns with the following labels: Time, Situation, Receiver Reaction, and My Feelings.

Then divide the paper into five rows. You probably want to number each row. Now throughout one day, pick five situations where you consciously decide to smile. Record your results. At the end of the day, assess the information.

Reflection Quote

The smile on your face is the light in the window that tells people you are home.

—Unknown

Smile Trial Worksheet

	Time	Situation	Receiver Reaction	My Feelings
1.				
2.				
3.				
4.				
5.				

Okay, judge. Were the results what you expected? Did the smiles affect the way you felt about yourself? How did they make others feel? You see, smiles really are magic—and you create it.

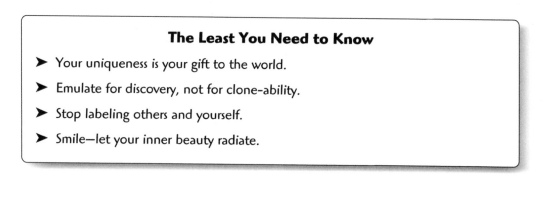

The Least You Need to Know

➤ Your uniqueness is your gift to the world.

➤ Emulate for discovery, not for clone-ability.

➤ Stop labeling others and yourself.

➤ Smile—let your inner beauty radiate.

Chapter 3

Embrace the Integrity Trinity

> ## In This Chapter
>
> ➤ Integrity intersections: Look before crossing
>
> ➤ Live the "Big 3"
>
> ➤ Promises, promises...
>
> ➤ Create the dream

Imagine this scenario. You open your morning newspaper and start reading the headlines. You say to yourself, "What would happen if I cut out all the articles that deal with someone's lack of integrity?" You cut and cut and cut. When you are finished, you realize that there is not much of the paper left—maybe a few comics, ads, and sports scores. Unfortunately, the vast majority of the paper addresses scandals, broken promises, cheating, stealing, and lying. Hmm.... We say that integrity is so important to us, and we use this as an excuse to comment constantly about the breaches of integrity that others commit. Our precious energy should not be expended on other peoples' integrity, but rather on what are we doing to enhance our own integrity. Integrity is the essence of who we are. It is the soul part of us, the center from which we make decisions. Our focus needs to stay within.

Integrity Intersections

Walk your talk. That phrase has resonated from boardrooms to classrooms, from churches and synagogues to political gatherings, from athletic fields to work cubicles, from homes to playgrounds. You've probably heard the phrase many times. For years, integrity experts have defined integrity as the intersection of behaviors and talk; the larger the intersection, the greater the integrity.

When you look at studies of what people want from their leaders and the significant others in their lives, integrity always heads the list. We want to be around people of integrity and we constantly default to our proven test to gauge whether someone is a person of integrity—does the person walk the talk? In fact, the only way for someone else to determine your integrity is for them to compare your actions and your words. Consistency shows integrity, incongruence points to a problem.

Unconventional Wisdom

Your true beauty is your integrity.

When you don't walk the talk, your credibility suffers, which in turn undermines your relationship with others. You owe it to yourself to match word and deed—the fruits will follow.

Walking your talk is a basic level of integrity, integrity as defined by others. As important as this order of integrity is, however, the challenge for us is to move to the highest level—the Integrity Trinity.

Integrity Trinity: The Highest Order

You are the only one on this earth who can truly judge your personal integrity—and this goes far beyond just assessing whether you walk your talk. In many instances, you can exhibit what looks like integrity but lack an essential element—belief. You can say things that are consistent with your actions without belief. Peer pressure and societal opinions can cause this to happen. For example, a politician might walk and talk the party line, but in his heart might not share these beliefs.

Reflection Quote

The ultimate measure of a man is not where he stands in moments of comfort and convenience, but where he stands at times of challenge and controversy.

—Martin Luther King, Jr.

Or consider the example of gang members. The talk is that they are the toughest and meanest. The behavior is inflicting pain on other people to establish turf. In this case, their words and behavior are in harmony. But inside, they often don't really believe that hurting another human being is the right thing to do: their belief is out of sync with their behavior and actions, because their need to belong overrides their convictions, and their integrity is compromised.

So how do you escape integrity impotence? Embrace the Integrity Trinity Formula. The *Integrity Trinity* is the intersection of words, deeds, *and* beliefs. When these three components are aligned, that is when the magic happens. You feel a sense of peace, a more solid sense of self, and an holistic integration of your personhood.

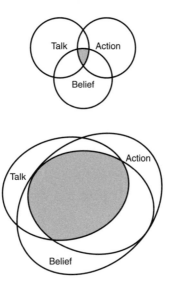

Integrity Trinity Reality, Small Intersection.

Integrity Trinity Goal, Large Intersection.

Resolution versus Promise

I'll share a little-known fact with you. Do you know why we use the phrase "New Year's Resolution" instead of "New Year's Promise"? Because we don't want to be liars in case we don't follow through. So what if I break a resolution? *Resolution* only means that I am determined to do something, which is much less significant than a promise. If I made a New Year's Promise, I might actually have to work to fulfill it. My guess is that if we made New Year's Promises, many more real behaviors would be changed.

Promises, Promises

We make a lot of promises—some to other people and some to ourselves. But we should all be more aware of the promises we make. After all, if you constantly break promises, people will lose respect for your word. Promise-making is serious business because promises have a direct impact on your own personal integrity. Use the following six points as important reminders.

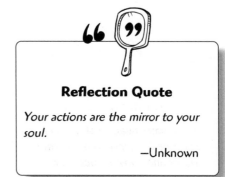

Reflection Quote

Your actions are the mirror to your soul.

—Unknown

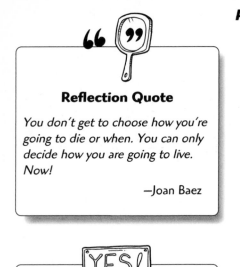

Reflection Quote

You don't get to choose how you're going to die or when. You can only decide how you are going to live. Now!

—Joan Baez

YES!

Power Plate

IB TRU2U

Promise-Making Common Sense

➤ Only make promises you can fulfill.

➤ Remember that promises you make to yourself are as important as promises you make to others.

➤ When fulfilling a promise to someone else, consciously make them aware that you are doing what you promised.

➤ Be a role model for others in the promise-keeping business.

➤ Let people know that promise-keeping is a value of yours.

➤ If for some reason you are unable to fulfill a promise, explain why and apologize to the person.

Promise-Keeping Check-up

Answer the following questions to give yourself a Promise-Keeping Check-up.

1. What is the last promise I made that I kept?

_____

_____

2. What kind of reaction did I get from the other person involved?

_____

_____

3. Did I know before I made the promise that I would actually be able to fulfill it?

_____

_____

4. How did I feel after I fulfilled the promise?

_____

_____

5. What is the last promise I made that I did not keep?

_____

_____

6. What kept me from fulfilling the promise?

_____

_____

7. How did the other person who was denied my promise feel?

_____

_____

8. Did I notify the person that I was not able to keep the promise? If so, how? Did I apologize? (If not, it is never too late to say you're sorry.)

_____

_____

9. How did being unable to keep the promise make me feel?

_____

_____

10. What did I learn from the experience?

_____

_____

Promise Checklist

Imagine that you are in the cockpit of a plane. Directly in front of you is a dashboard crammed full of gauges, switches, and buttons. You have been given pilot status complete with your own aviator glasses and your favorite leather flight jacket. (I hope the jacket fits!) Before you get this winged piece of metal into the air, you are obligated to go through a series of checklists to ensure that you have made all the safety checks and preflight decisions that will enable you to have a successful journey. Your checklist is the key to success and survival.

There is another kind of checklist that is the key to your success and survival—a promise-making checklist. Unfortunately many times people make promises on the spot, spontaneously, rather than as a result of a thoughtful approach. This is when promises are made that should never have been made.

So here's a Promises Checklist to help you out. The checklist is based on four questions:

Reflection Quote

Your conscience is the measure of the honesty of your selfishness. Listen to it carefully.

—Richard Bach

Power Plate

NTEGRT

1. What are my motives for making the promise?
2. Will I be able to fulfill the promise?
3. Does the promise represent who I truly am?
4. In terms of magnitude, is this a big or little promise?

Let's look at these questions in a checklist format. Choose a promise you are considering and glide through the checklist.

➤ What are my motives for making the promise?
- ❏ I want to impress the person.
- ❏ I really want to help the person.
- ❏ I can't say "no" to anyone.
- ❏ I want to make the other person feel good.
- ❏ I like the feeling of power that comes with promise-making.

➤ Will I be able to fulfill the promise?
- ❏ I have the resources to fulfill the promise (money, knowledge, tools, for example).
- ❏ I have the authority to fulfill the promise.
- ❏ I have the will-power to follow through.

➤ Does the promise represent who I truly am?
- ❏ The promise is consistent with my beliefs.
- ❏ The promise is consistent with my behaviors.
- ❏ The promise is consistent with my talk.

➤ In terms of magnitude, is this a big or little promise?
- ❏ It is a small promise that I can deal with immediately.
- ❏ It is a small promise that I can fulfill by myself.
- ❏ It is a small promise, but I will still need to get help from others.
- ❏ It is a big promise that may take some time to fulfill.
- ❏ It is a big promise that I will need to get help from others to fulfill.
- ❏ It is a big promise, but I will still be able to handle it myself.

Now, based on all this information, do I make the promise?

_____ YES

_____ NO

Live the Dream

Dreams. Nocturnal motion pictures. Sometimes in color, sometimes in black and white. Often surreal, often *too* real. But these nighttime mind-nudgers are much less important than the conscious dreaming we employ, addressing our futures—who do I want to become? What do I want to accomplish? How do I want to make a difference in the life of another person? These are dreams that have to do with personal integrity and a sense of self.

When I think about dreams, I'm reminded of an experience I had with my daughter Sarah when she was six years old. We went to the park to fly a kite. After about 30 minutes of trying to get the kite in flight, we finally succeeded. We were lying in the grass, looking up at the kite, and after several minutes of quiet reflection, young Sarah said, "Dad, when you look at the kite, the blue sky and the white clouds, it fills your mind with dreams." Hmm.... Wisdom from the mouth of a child. It's time to listen.

We must constantly have dreams, for they propel us into future opportunities, experiences, and growth. While recognizing the importance of realizing a specific dream, we must remind ourselves that any single dream is only part of the journey, a signpost on the road of life. When we fulfill one dream, it's time to venture down another path in search of other dreams. Dreaming is a perpetual activity that enriches the spirit and adds luster to your life.

Dreams must be acted on. Otherwise, they are just beautiful images painted by the mind. The action is the hard part, because we have to figure out "how to get there from here." The expedition can be fraught with naysayers and obstacles. No one said that this dreaming business was easy. If your dream is authentic, however, you will be able to draw from your incredible internal resources, which will enable you to conquer the fear, disregard the detractors, and mobilize the synergy forces of mind, body, and spirit—you then will fulfill your aspirations.

Unconventional Wisdom

Do you ever find yourself keeping promises you make to other people more than the promises you make to yourself? Why is that? The reality is that the more promises to yourself you keep, the more you'll keep for others.

Reflection Quote

We live in deeds, not years; in thoughts, not breaths; in feelings, not in figures on a dial. We should count time by heart throbs. The person most lives who thinks most, feels the noblest, acts the best.

—*Phillip James Bailey*

Inspirational Injection

Dream Big

If there were ever a time to dare,

to make a difference,

to embark on something worth doing,

it is now.

Not for any grand cause, necessarily—

but for something that tugs at your heart,

something that's your aspiration,

something that's your dream.

You owe it to yourself

to make your days here count.

Have fun.

Dig deep.

Stretch.

Dream Big.

Know, though that things worth doing

seldom come easy.

There will be good days.

There will be bad days.

There will be times when you want to turn around,

pack it up,

and call it quits.

Those times tell you

that you are pushing yourself,

that you are not afraid to learn by trying.

Persist.

Because with an idea,

determination,

and the right tools,

you can do great things.

Let your instincts, your intellect, and your heart guide you.

Trust.

Believe in the incredible power of the human kind.

Of doing something that makes a difference.

Of working hard.

Of laughing and hoping.

Of lazy afternoons.

Of lasting friends.

Of all the things that will cross your path this year.

The start of something new

brings the hope of something great.

Anything is possible.

There is only one you.

And you will pass this way only once.

Do it right.

Dream Big.

—Unknown

Front-Burner Dreams

You sacrifice for your children, you sacrifice for your significant others, you sacrifice for your community—you put your own dreams on the back burner. You may think you're being noble when you put your dreams on hold, but by doing so you are stealing from your own reservoir of riches. You deny yourself emotional and spiritual gifts that would add wonder and excitement to your life. When you put your dreams on the front burner, however, your transformed self enables you to touch the lives of others more effectively. The result of creating your dreams in tandem with others is energized, exhilarated living.

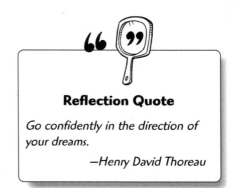

Reflection Quote

Go confidently in the direction of your dreams.

—Henry David Thoreau

The Least You Need to Know

➤ Integrate beliefs, talk, and action.

➤ Be a promise keeper.

➤ Make calculated promises.

➤ Dream to live and live to dream.

Part 2
Risk Taking:
Become a Change Hugger

The less of routine, the more of life.

A. B. Alcott

As we all know, change can be intimidating. But sometimes we resist change so much that we begin to stagnate. You need to learn how to start building change into your life. This means adopting a new perspective on life, giving yourself permission to make mistakes, and learning how to assess risks and make use of the ones you decide are worthwhile. It also means facing fear directly! As you confront fear, you'll begin to see how it can be a catalyst of change and focus.

Chapter 4

Champion Change Courageously

Here is a standardized test question. Which of the following phrases does not fit?

   a. Change a light-bulb.

   b. Change your clothes.

   c. Change a tire.

   d. Change a life.

   e. Change the linens.

   f. Change a diaper.

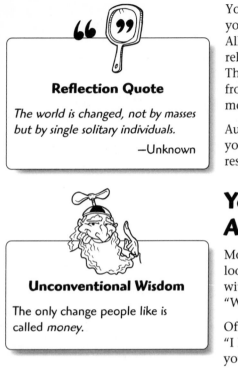

Reflection Quote

The world is changed, not by masses but by single solitary individuals.

—Unknown

Unconventional Wisdom

The only change people like is called *money*.

You're right—"d"—Change a life! Did you guess or did you use that great combination of intuition and reason? All the other phrases describe one-time activities that are relatively easy (except maybe the diaper changing). These activities are low-risk and essentially divorced from our sense of self. But changing a life is one of the most difficult life tasks we can ever encounter.

Authentic change requires the holistic synergy force of your body, mind, and spirit. No wonder people initially resist change.

You Can Be a Change Architect

Most people look forward to change as much as they look forward to stepping on a tack. When confronted with change, you might be like most of us who say, "Why *me*?!"

Of course, some of you reading this might be thinking "I love change. I thrive on change." But if this is you, you're definitely in a minority. Count your blessings.

How do you answer these questions?

1. When was the most recent time you changed? One year ago? One month ago? One week ago? One day ago? Today?

   _____

   _____

2. How did you change?

   _____

   _____

3. Are most of your life changes initiated by you or by others?

   _____

   _____

Inspirational Injection

Man alone, of all the creatures of the earth, can change his own pattern. Man alone is the architect of his destiny. The greatest discovery in our generation is that human beings, by changing the inner attitudes of their minds, can change the outer aspects of their lives.

—William James

Let's look at the answers to these questions. I would venture to say that the most recent change for all of us happened today! We usually only consider the big, momentous events as change. But in reality, what really changes who we are comes from our daily experiences and our reactions to them. This is called *personal creation*, and personal creation means change.

Okay. Question #2. Are most of your changes initiated by you or by others? If you said that you initiate most of your life changes, then you probably feel a greater sense of control over your life. If you said "others," then you may feel less in control—more acted upon than taking action.

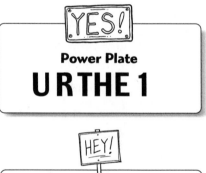

Power Plate

URTHE 1

The key is to become the initiator, to take more control of your life by making choices, by creating yourself. Remember, you create your life, your change—no one else does.

There are two universal change concepts that have been expounded throughout the ages. I think they probably were the original hieroglyphics Og wrote on the cave wall and used as the argument in favor of using fire. People examining the issue of change have incorporated Og's rules ever since:

Here are Og's two simple rules.

1. You can be your own change creator or you can be the victim of change.

2. Change is the only consistent aspect of humankind.

Action Prompt

Think of someone—a friend or relative—who at some point in your life was very important to you but became separated from you for some reason (moving or circumstances). Now give that person a call, just to say "hi." By taking this one small step, you can rekindle a relationship—even if only for an instant. You can create a change moment.

Og does rule! Although philosophers have grappled with these rules for centuries, even today they remain the rules for change.

New Eyes Ceremony

Think about your living room. Imagine the pictures you have hung on the walls. (I'll give you a second to do your imagining.) My guess is that if you have lived in

that place for more than six months, you don't even see the pictures anymore when you walk into the room.

Why is that? It's something that happens to your brain. You've walked by the pictures so many times that your brain does not click on to acknowledge them—the pictures have lost their stimulus power.

It's the same thing with other aspects of our lives. When we do things the same way we've always done them, the brain becomes numb and we tend to get results similar to those of past endeavors.

> **Unconventional Wisdom**
>
> The only difference between a rut and the grave is the dimensions.
>
> —Unknown

Take the Oath

In order to stimulate the ol' brain and prevent the numbness, you need a new set of eyes. I know you are thinking—"What? Has Mark lost his mind?"

Nope—new eyes are the solution. You don't get these eyes free, however. You have to repeat an oath. But wait—we can't start the oath yet. It comes with some choreography. Let's practice. Touch your index finger to your thumb on each hand and form two small circles. Now put the two circles up to your eyes. These are your new eyes.

Okay. Ready for the oath? With your new eyes in proper choreographic position, repeat the following:

> **Reflection Quote**
>
> *The real voyage of discovery consists not in seeking new landscapes, but in having new eyes.*
>
> —Marcel Proust

Today I have a new pair of eyes,

Eyes that will help me see my role in life differently.

I have great potential, and...

Now is the time

To seek questions, challenges, and opportunities.

And by making a commitment to optimal living,

I can make a difference.

You may put your new eyes down now. Do you know what the wonderful thing is about these new eyes you just received? They're portable. You can put them in your pockets, you can take them in the shower—wherever you go, they can be with you.

The hard part, however, is that you have to consciously put them on. In order to make a difference in your life and in the world, you have to look at it through different lenses.

Assess Your Behavior

Think for a moment about what you have done today. What behaviors are basically repeats of the way you have done things before? Write down three of these behaviors, and your response to them, following this example:

> Action: I commuted to work and gazed out the window for the 30-minute metro ride.
>
> Response: I watched life go by while I traveled to work.

1. Action:

   Response:

2. Action:

   Response:

3. Action:

   Response:

Why do you repeat the actions? What purpose does the repetition serve?

_____

_____

Take the three actions you listed and this time, following the example, identify some optional behaviors you could employ (either variations on established behaviors or brand-new behaviors):

> Action: I commuted to work and read a great book to enhance my potential.
>
> Response: I got some ideas for a few new things I can try, and became energized for the day.

1. Action:

   Response:

2. Action:

   Response:

3. Action:

   Response:

Unconventional Wisdom

Someone once told me, "I love change; I just don't like being changed!"

I realize that changing the particular behaviors you identify just to appease me might not change your life. But I think you get the point. You can enrich your life by assessing what you do routinely and by trying different behaviors. This practice will help you jump-start your brain. The key is that this is a continual process—not a one-time effort. You will notice a difference.

Lesson of the Pine Caterpillar

You learn from experience. You learn from people. You learn from education. How about from a pine caterpillar? Yes, our long, hairy, ground-bound friend that cavorts around conifers (that's pine trees, for the nonnaturalist reader).

Years ago I was reading about individual success and I bumped into "The Lesson of the Pine Caterpillar." I learned this lesson from the writings of Dr. Keith DeGreen.

The pine caterpillar is about an inch long, has an abundance of legs, is earthy in color, and has some serious feelers. It boasts an accordion-shaped body that slowly gets it from place to place. Its physical features are interesting to look at, but its behaviors are even more fascinating.

Do you know what happens when you put these caterpillars end to end to form a circle, then put food in the middle of the circle? First of all, it is no easy task to get them end to end. It takes an entomologist with many years of education to perform this procedure. In the next room you can just hear the scientist with the white lab coat on, issuing scientific commands: "Here caterpillar, here caterpillar. Let's form a circle."

Here is what happens when you have caterpillars in a circle with food in the middle. They will go 'round and 'round and 'round…until they starve to death. They don't have imaginations, they are not innovative, and they cannot take a risk to get out of the circle, even when their lives depend upon it.

Do you ever develop a pine caterpillar mentality? Sure—we all do. Sometimes it is when fear and uncertainty present themselves. Friends of the pine caterpillar mentality abound. Sometimes Fatigue forges into the limelight. Sometimes Insecurity surfaces. Then Lack-of-Self-Confidence rears its ugly head. Hmm. These don't sound like friends to me.

The pine caterpillar mentality is a powerful condition. Luckily, there are some great insect repellents on the market. I happen to favor the natural, environmentally safe varieties. Here's one potent repellent specifically designed for this phenomenon.

Unconventional Wisdom

Our classroom is the world before us, within us, and around us.

Action Prompt

Reflect for a moment on your primary response to change. Get in touch with that feeling. Today, when change greets you, instead of looking at it as a threat, welcome it as an opportunity. Ask yourself, "How can I use this for growth?" Then take one action step to move yourself in a positive direction.

Pine Caterpillar–Mentality Repellent

This repellent is FDA (Fantastic Developmental Attitude) approved and harmless to plants, vegetables, and animals. It is effective in large doses. If first application does not work, then repeated applications will be necessary.

Directions for Use:

It is in violation of Federal law to use this product in a manner inconsistent with its labeling. For use early in life, in midlife, and later in life. At some points in life you may need stronger doses. You have total control over the impact this product will have on you. Do not use sparingly.

Active Ingredients:

Myopic commitment to helping others...21%

Polyuntainted propensity to personal growth..19%

Undiluted proactive life orientation..17%

Double-strength "You Make a Difference" belief..24%

Concentrate of being comfortable with your discomfort.......................................<u>19%</u>

Total...100%

CAUTION:

Pine Caterpillar Mentality strengthens if not treated. Prevention is the best repellent.

Discomfort Is Not the Enemy

Discomfort tells us something is wrong. Discomfort is bad. Right? *Wrong!* Actually, discomfort can propel you onto positive paths. When you're hungry, you are **discomfortable**, so you eat. When you're cold, you are **dis**comfortable, so you put on a jacket. Discomfort serves as an important and necessary catalyst for action—for change.

We are taught early in life a distinct physiological lesson about discomfort: *avoid* it. But instead of avoiding it, try asking yourself, "Why the discomfort? What is the root of the discomfort?" If you go to the root, then you will gain the learning. If you look only at the symptoms, growth will be thwarted.

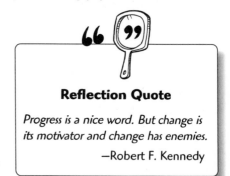

Reflection Quote

Progress is a nice word. But change is its motivator and change has enemies.

—Robert F. Kennedy

I'm not saying to go out and look for discomfort. That's called *masochism*, and you don't want to be accused of that. I am, however, suggesting that you use the positive benefits of discomfort to create an optimal life.

Change Is a Feeling

Change is all about feelings—physical and emotional. Let's try something. Look down at your wristwatch. It is a fine watch, isn't it? I'm sure it has shared some adventures with you and could probably tell some stories—but we won't go there.

Take off your wristwatch and put it on the other wrist. How does that feel?

➤ Strange?

➤ Awkward?

➤ Uncomfortable?

In fact, your first reaction might be: "Whoa, I've got to get this back to the correct wrist, where it belongs."

That is how change feels. At times strange, awkward, and uncomfortable. You want to go back to what is comfortable. This is a common ingredient of the human condition.

But you can work past the desire to go back to the old way. You can learn to feel comfortable with the wristwatch on the new wrist, with a little time and a commitment to change.

It is the same in other aspects of life. The essence of dealing effectively with change is your reaction to change, whether initiated by you or not. You must give yourself permission to experience change, feel change, and grow from change. When you control change (which sounds like an oxymoron, right?), you do create your life, minute by minute.

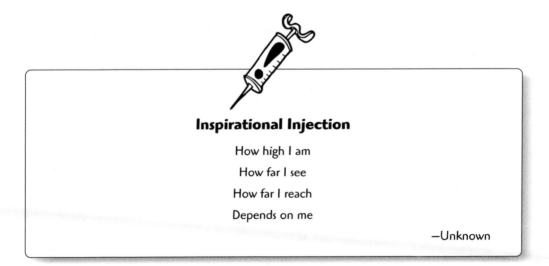

Inspirational Injection

How high I am

How far I see

How far I reach

Depends on me

—Unknown

The Stagnation Factor

Imagine that you are walking through the woods on a beautiful summer day. Lush vegetation and the music of wildlife greet you. You walk down a trail, exhilarated by the gift of nature. Then you look to your left and see something that just isn't right.

Before you is a small body of water. It emits an unpleasant odor. You see insects hovering over a brownish-green film that cloaks the surface of the water. The water is so foul that you cannot imagine how anything could live in there—stagnant water becomes smelly and lifeless.

What you are viewing is stagnation at its finest. Does your life ever become stagnant? Do you ever just exist? Is your life ever so stationary that you become covered with a film? I hope not.

Unfortunately, too many people live the stagnant life. Have you ever run into someone who simply drudges through each day, hoping to make it to the next day to once again drudge on, settling for a stagnated existence?

You can get rid of your stagnation. Invite the rushing waters of change into your life and enjoy their cleansing powers. Appreciate the exhilaration that new perspectives and new experiences will bring. By doing this you can grow instead of decay. The life you change will be *yours*.

Power Plate

LIF–C2IT

Unconventional Wisdom

Resisting change drains energy. Embracing change creates energy. You choose.

The Least You Need to Know

➤ You create yourself day by day, hour by hour, minute by minute.

➤ You can influence change and its effect on your life.

➤ Change can be an ally or a foe...you choose.

➤ Discomfort can provoke positive change—if you let it.

Heads, I take a shot, Tails, I take a different shot...

Chapter 5

Random Rules for Risk Taking

In This Chapter

➤ Learning the importance of giving permission

➤ Going to school on your mistakes

➤ Why calculating is a must

➤ Mastering the matrix

Swim…at your own risk.

Parasail…at your own risk.

Rock climb…at your own risk.

Have you ever seen signs like these? Basically what they mean is—*you* decide. Actually, everything you do could use the qualifier "…at your own risk," like:

➤ Get a job…at your own risk.

➤ Get married…at your own risk.

➤ Go to college…at your own risk.

➤ Eat toastee-oats…at your own risk.

Life is…at your own risk. The irony is that risk is one of the greatest gifts we were given at birth. Risk is a lifetime gift that allows us to create ourselves.

Decree "Permission to Make Mistakes Day"

Reflection Quote

A ship in the harbor is safe—but that is not what ships are for.

—John A. Shedd

Today you are given an awesome responsibility. For some reason you have been tapped to be the Head Calendar Creator, and your magic allows you to determine which days should be special days.

As you peruse the current calendar and examine the special days that already exist, you discover days like:

➤ Mother's Day

➤ Valentine's Day

➤ Groundhog Day

Reflection Quote

Learn from the mistakes of others. You don't have time to make them all yourself.

—Unknown

You realize that it is no easy task to be the day designator—there are so many people and things worth commemorating. Well, I'm going to help you out. Here is a day that has gone unrecognized for too long. May I have the envelope please? The enclosed message reads:

PERMISSION TO MAKE MISTAKES DAY

As you read this message a little closer you realize that this day is not like others. The fine print encourages you to acknowledge this day every day of your life—not one special day a year, not one special day a month, but every single day of the year.

The Mistake Reality

The reality of being human is that you will make mistakes. Unfortunately, sometimes our self-protection genes kick in and ask us to deny, cover up, or not face our mistakes. At least that happens to me. Does it ever happen to you?

Action Prompt

"I can't wait until..."

"I can't wait until..."

"I can't wait until..."

Hmm. Don't wait. Do it now.

What would really happen if you gave yourself permission to make mistakes? Imagine the benefits:

➤ A whole new world opens up before you.

➤ You take more risks.

➤ You allow yourself to be vulnerable—in a positive way.

➤ You expose yourself to more life adventures.

➤ You grow as a person.

➤ You create antibodies against perfectionism.

If you give yourself permission to make mistakes, does that mean that you wake up and say, "All right world, I'm going to go out and make some mistakes today"? No, that's not what I'm talking about. What I'm talking about is waking up and saying, "I'm going to look for some opportunities today. I'm going to try some new things. I'm going to create my day."

Get a Ph.D. in Mistake Making

Ahh, to be a student again.

Do you want to earn a Ph.D? This one you don't even have to get from a mail-order house. The diploma— made of sheepish skin—is of course conferred, of course, only after you have met the criteria.

Your classroom is called *life*. The core curriculum centers on mistakes. Yikes! And there is a fundamental concept you need to consider before starting to pursue this degree; mistakes create the essence.

You can be either a student of your mistakes or a victim of them—you and you alone choose. If you choose the student option, then your Ph.D. is just a few short classes away.

As a human being, you are a learning creature by nature and design. When you look at mistakes as teachers, you can enhance your own sense of self.

Some of the greatest learning experiences in your life probably came from mistakes you made. At the time I'll bet you didn't say, "I sure am glad I'm having this learning experience." In fact, the experience might have been very painful. The learning comes later, when you make a conscious effort to reflect back, and when you ask yourself "What can I learn from this?"

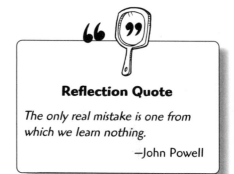

Reflection Quote

The only real mistake is one from which we learn nothing.

—John Powell

Mistake-Making Curriculum

Mistake-making, like any legitimate Ph.D. program, has a specified curriculum. Here it is, but only if you're ready for the challenge.

Mistake-Making Ph.D. Curriculum

Course Title	Course Description
MM 101. History of Mistake Making	Discover the great mistakes from Caveperson Og to Edison to your neighbor next door.

continues

continued

Course Title	Course Description
MM 102. Psychology of Mistake Making	Learn how you feel about making mistakes and why.
MM 103. Practicum in Mistake Making	Otherwise known as *life*.
MM 104. Mistake-Making Techniques	You will be exposed to techniques ranging from the nuances of strategic subtle mistakes to grand blunders.
MM 105. Mistake-Making Theories	He did it, she did it, we did it. Examine the theories of how and why.
MM 106. Mistake Making: the Personal Side	Your mistakes are uniquely you. Learn through introspection.

Sign up for your courses today!

Smart Risks: Make the Time Investment

Every summer our family goes to the beach for our vacation. We wallow in the sand, tumble in the waves, and partake in a beach adventure—the local kite shop climbing wall. It simulates rock climbing, at least for everyone except real rock climbers.

The folks who operate the wall are big on safety. They equip us with climbing shoes, karabiners, ropes, and helmets (we also sign a "don't sue the company" note). What was once a risky enterprise is now much safer: although there is still some risk, it is a calculated risk.

Suppose, however, you decide to climb the wall without the appropriate protective gear. This is also a risk, but not a smart one. The consequences could be grave.

In life, you are bombarded by the words of others imploring you to take risks. The key is to take smart, calculated risks. This is the secret of making risk-taking growth-producing not fatal.

Inspirational Injection

To laugh is to risk appearing the fool.

To weep is to risk appearing sentimental.

To reach out for another is to risk involvement.

To expose feelings is to risk expressing one's true self.

To place your ideas, your dreams, before the crowd is to risk loss.

To love is to risk not being loved in return.

To live is to risk dying.

To hope is to risk despair.

To try at all is to risk failure.

But risk we must, because the great hazard in life is to risk nothing.

The man, the woman, who risks nothing, does nothing, has nothing, is nothing.

—Unknown

So, what questions can help you assess the amount of risk you are willing to take? Here are some of them:

➤ What are the long-term consequences of the risk?

➤ What are the short-term consequences of the risk?

➤ What are the costs? (financial, time, emotional)

➤ Who can help me assess the risks involved?

➤ What homework can I do to help me decide?

➤ Is the risk consistent with my values?

➤ What are the risks involved with *not* taking this risk?

What other questions can you ask yourself?

_____

_____

_____

Risk Assessment: A Solo Endeavor? Not!

Too often when we are confronted with some type of risk-taking scenario, we feel that we have to make the decision independently or without feedback from others. In fact, the opposite is true. We ought to get as much input as we can from others.

Power Plate

CALQL8

Here are some of the benefits of input from others:

➤ Different perspectives

➤ Additional knowledge and experience base

➤ Objective viewpoints

➤ Rich understandings

If you are not willing to or don't give yourself permission to seek input from others, you run the risk of contracting Myopic Risk-Assessment Disease. You won't have the information necessary to make the best decision. Reach out, take in, weigh the information, and decide.

Action Prompt

Think of an idea that you have been wanting to explore. Seek out someone you respect and say, "I've got this idea. Here it is. I respect your input. What am I not considering? Are there other things I should be considering? Do you see any holes in it?" Take the input and go to the next step, which is action.

Calculate: The Non-Mathematical Way

What was one of the first calculations you ever learned? Probably $1 + 1 = 2$. When you first learned it, you discovered a whole new world. The great part about this new bit of knowledge was that whenever anyone asked you what $1 + 1$ was, you had the correct answer.

Wouldn't it be great if calculating our life risks were that easy? Throw a few factors into a formula, have the computer giggle a bit, then wait for *the* answer. As we know, however, life just doesn't work that way.

I wonder what would happen if we were able to come up with precise answers, if we took all of the suspense out of risk taking and making. How would that affect us? Would we be the beneficiaries of the same type of growth? Would we be able to make the same kind of life contribution?

Risks are part of our lives because we *need* risks. Risks bring a thrill, an expectation, a hope. If the unknown were always known, then the concepts of hope and anticipation would not be the powerful soul-creating agents they are.

Unconventional Wisdom

The purpose of hope is not to create a better tomorrow, but to create a better today. If you live today to the fullest, then tomorrow will take care of itself.

50

Risk-Taking Matrix Query

So you're ready for some risks? Then it's time for the query. Let these steps be your guide:

1. Identify the risk.
2. If low risk, then trust your intuition and go for it.
3. If medium to high risk, then use the Risk-Taking Matrix Query below.

Competence and support are the essential partners of successful risk taking. These qualities form the axis of the quadrant components:

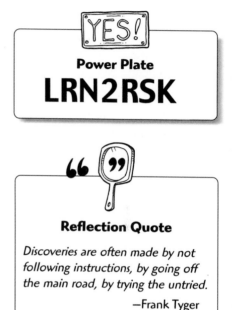

Power Plate

LRN2RSK

Reflection Quote

Discoveries are often made by not following instructions, by going off the main road, by trying the untried.

—Frank Tyger

➤ **Competence.** Either you have the ability to do what you set out to do or surround yourself with others who have the ability.

➤ **Support.** External and internal support are needed. External support includes such items as material and financial resources and physical, moral, and intellectual assistance. Internal support can be based upon your own intuition or upon the knowledge that you know what you are risking is the right thing to do.

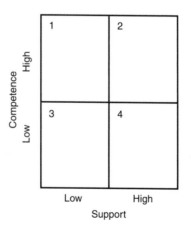

Quadrant 1: High Competence/Low Support. If you're seriously considering this risk, you need to boost the support level. Find out why support is lacking. Reassess if necessary. **Action:** Boost support.

Quadrant 2: High Competence/High Support. You are ready to take the risk.
Action: Go for it!

Quadrant 3:. Low Competence/Low Support. You're not ready. You know it and *they* know it. **Action:** Respectfully decline. In other words—Forget it!

Quadrant 4:. Low Competence/High Support. You've got the cheerleaders, but something else is lacking: skill. You've got to enhance the competence factor. Either build your own competence or surround yourself with others who are competent. **Action:** Boost confidence.

OK. Let's try the Matrix Query:

Matrix Query

1. Identify a risk:

   _____

   _____

2. Identify the appropriate quadrant. Answer the questions for each quadrant to see where the best fit is:

   _____

   _____

3. What action do I need to take?

   _____

   _____

4. Next steps:

   _____

   _____

The Least You Need to Know

➤ Mistakes are an essential part of growth.

➤ Resources abound to help you with risk-taking decisions.

➤ A little risk assessment goes a long way.

➤ Learn from mistakes for success, ignore for failure.

Chapter 6

Deep-Six the Fear Factor

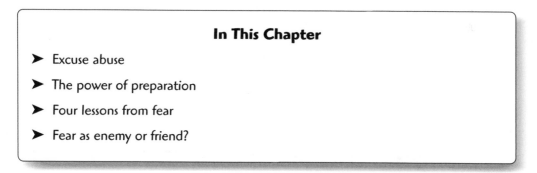

In This Chapter

➤ Excuse abuse

➤ The power of preparation

➤ Four lessons from fear

➤ Fear as enemy or friend?

Too often, fear puts people in graves before they've ever lived. *R.I.P.* the tombstone reads: "rest in peace." Let's get rid of the R.I.P. and make it an *L.I.P.* What? L.I.P.—live in peace. The best way to live in peace is to deal with the fear factor. Sometimes that means deep-sixin' it, and other times it means using it to your benefit. The challenge is to figure out which course to take when. No easy task, but the rewards are great.

Excuses: Means of Maintaining Mediocrity

Think about what happens when someone asks you to change or take a risk. Immediately the engines of discomfort start churning, which in turn engage the sprockets that generate excuses.

Excuses, excuses, excuses! When do excuses drip from our lips? Try these on for size:

➤ When we don't want to accept responsibility

➤ When we don't want to be held accountable

➤ When we don't want to face reality

➤ When we want to avoid something

➤ When we want to deceive ourselves (or others)

➤ When we want a scapegoat

➤ When we're afraid

Harsh reality, isn't it?!

The problem with excuses is that they promote mediocrity. And when you embrace and accept mediocrity, you marginalize yourself. By the way, no one else can marginalize you—only you can. That's one scapegoat you have to let escape.

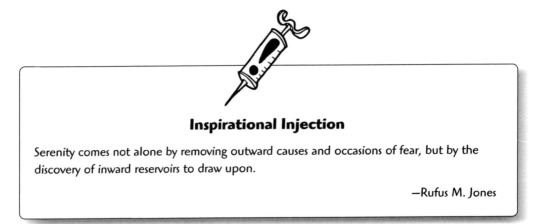

Inspirational Injection

Serenity comes not alone by removing outward causes and occasions of fear, but by the discovery of inward reservoirs to draw upon.

—Rufus M. Jones

We are all great excuse makers, especially when discomfort greets us. What are some of the excuses you use when you don't want to take a risk, when you don't want to change?

Don't answer yet. Let me change the question: What are some of the excuses "a friend" might use when confronted with change? (I hope you feel better now.)

In seminars and classes I've conducted on this topic, I've heard a fairly common list. My guess is that your "friend's" list might include some of these:

➤ I've always done it that way.

➤ There is not enough time.

➤ There is not enough money.

➤ I don't want to.

➤ It's okay as it is.

➤ Why?

➤ It might not work.

➤ There is no support for change.

➤ I might make a mistake.

Can you add some others?

➤ _____

➤ _____

➤ _____

Reduce the Big F

Although excuses abound, the bottom line is that they all revolve around *the Big F*. Yes, the Big F. You know what the Big F stands for, don't you? You're right—'Fraid. (Oh well, so you said Fear. I'll let it go this time.)

Fear does have an important role to play in your life. It was designed to assist you in self-protection. A noble mechanism indeed, as long as it doesn't propagate paralysis.

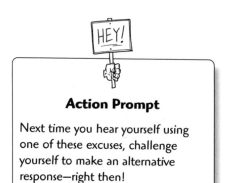

Action Prompt

Next time you hear yourself using one of these excuses, challenge yourself to make an alternative response—right then!

Real versus Imaginary

When you were young you probably had an imaginary friend. Your friend was there for you—to play with you, to comfort you, to support you. You probably moved away from that imaginary friend years ago—didn't you?

We laugh about imaginary friends, but it is not so funny when we talk about imaginary enemies—and we still have those today as adults. One is named *Fear*. Do you ever find him sharing time with you, competing with your sense of security, or creeping uninvited into your thoughts and actions?

My guess is that he is a more frequent visitor at some points in your life than at others. And sometimes he is probably easier to shoo away.

So let's get this straight—sometimes fear is a self-protector and at other times fear is an enemy. How do I realize which fear I'm confronting?

Inspirational Injection

ICARUS

Last night I dreamed of Icarus
And how he flew too high
With wax and feathers for his wings
He tried to touch the sky.
And some say
   When we soar with pride
And lack humility
An angry God reminds us
Of the laws of gravity.

Last night I dreamed of Challenger
And seven souls who dared
How fire hurled them back to earth
And not one life was spared.
And some say
   There's a secret vision
Only God should see
So we should stay here
   Bound to Earth
And let the heavens be.

But I say
   When we try and fail
And dare to try once more
Something lives
   Within our hearts
That wasn't there before.
And where our reach
   Exceeds our grasp
Fantastic worlds begin
We touch the gates of heaven
And God invites us in.

Last night I dreamed of children
Who believe that they can fly
Who travel their imaginations
Far beyond the sky
Like Icarus,
   The Challengers
Are never dead and gone
They're always waiting somewhere
To cheer the children on.

—Jack Presbury

Be F.A.R. Sighted

If you are going to be able to effectively discern which face of fear you're staring at, you need to be F.A.R. sighted—Fear Assessment Responsive. You have to open yourself up to some tough questions. This is the only way you'll know how to deal with the fear.

Let's look at the assessment through a personal example so that it will be more meaningful to you.

1. Identify a decision you are facing that causes you fear.

   _____

   _____

2. Does this fear threaten your physical safety? If so, how? And what can you do to reduce the threat?

   _____

   _____

3. Does this fear threaten your emotional security? If so, how? And what can you do to reduce the threat?

   _____

   _____

4. If you decide to take the action, what are the potential negative consequences?

   _____

   _____

5. If you decide to take the action, what are the potential positive consequences?

   _____

   _____

6. Is the fear real or imagined?

   _____

   _____

7. From whom can you garner support in dealing with the fear?

   _____

   _____

8. What does your intuition tell you to do?

_____

_____

9. What does your logic tell you to do?

_____

_____

10. Who else does this decision impact?

_____

_____

11. Fooled you. You thought this was a question. No. However, it is the next step.

_____

_____

Now that you've answered these 10 questions, I encourage you to open your calendar and flip to the day that is 48 hours from now (that's two days, for those of you who are mathematically challenged). On that date, write a note to yourself to revisit the questions. These two days give your subconscious a chance to work its magic. It also allows you to address the questions with a new perspective.

By taking a proactive stance in working with the fear in your life, you can partner with it rather than being ruled by it. Also, the more you take yourself through the assessment process, the easier the process becomes—and as a result, the easier the decision.

The Preparation Factor

Praeparare. Okay, Latin lovers, help us out with this word. If we break it down into its components, we know that *prae* means before and *parare* means make ready. When we put the two together, we come up with "make ready before." Or, if we want to get out of the old world language mode we can slip into the more familiar English vernacular—it means to prepare.

When you think about it, preparation can have an enormous impact on your life. In fact, preparation has a dual benefit:

1. Preparation reduces fear.

2. Preparation increases the opportunity for success.

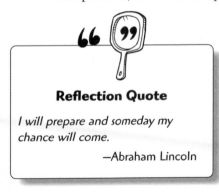

Reflection Quote

I will prepare and someday my chance will come.

—Abraham Lincoln

So how do you prepare yourself? There are myriad ways. I'll give you just a few.

➤ Practice.

➤ Do your homework.

➤ Anticipate obstacles.

➤ Use all your resources (colleagues, friends, family, Internet…).

➤ Learn from others.

➤ Get different perspectives.

➤ Pray or meditate.

➤ Relax, to keep your perspective and to reduce tension.

➤ Listen.

Preparation is the foundation for skill development. It is the antidote to fear and the essential ingredient for success.

Success Is Luck—Not!

Many times people will say that someone is successful because of luck. I don't believe in luck. My favorite definition of luck is from Elmer Letterman (no relation to David), who says, "Luck is what happens when preparation meets opportunity."

Hmm…. Interesting concept. In effect, what happens is that preparation becomes a magnet that attracts opportunities. The more opportunities you have, the more options you have. The more options you have, the more fruitful your life can become. Don't curse options, embrace them.

Your success will be dictated by preparation, not by luck. Create your luck today.

Reflection Quote

Courage is fear that has said its prayers.

—Unknown

Unconventional Wisdom

Preparation reduces risks, creates opportunities, and enhances potential for success.

From 'Fraidy Cat to Adventurous Aardvark

"'Fraidy Feline. 'Fraidy Feline. Thyself doth dare ye to make it so." Those words echoed throughout the courtyards of Elizabethan England. But as language so often does, this expression has changed over the centuries. Thoughts of our own childhood bring back memories of an updated version of the taunting, which goes something like this:

"'Fraidy Cat, 'Fraidy Cat. I dare you to do it."

Times might change the words, but the intent stays the same. Those were the horrifying words our peers would use to coerce us into doing something we didn't want to do—for whatever reason. Usually the reason had something to do with fear.

Think about how different things would have been if our playground pals had yelled "Adventurous Aardvark, Adventurous Aardvark—you can do it!" Boy, would our experience have been different.

Back to the point. There *are* times when we do need to say no, when we should listen to the fear. Coercion, whether overt or covert, is not an acceptable motivator for taking action. You have to choose for yourself what level of risk you are willing to take. Fear is the stimulus to ask the questions, and the answers help make the decisions. Without fear, you might not ask the questions and might find yourself playing with peril.

Reflection Quote

Maturity is not a state one suddenly arrives at. It is a continuous development, achieved less by age than by insight.

—Michael Drury

Let's go back to the Adventurous Aardvark. Sure, you would like to be awarded this title, complete with credentials that grant you the rights and privileges of one so designated. That's great. But don't be a foolish Aardvark, acting on impulse and without proper consideration of the consequences.

'Fraidy Cat—*no*. Adventurous Aardvark—*maybe*. Sound decision-maker—*yes!*

Make Fear an Ally

Put up your dukes or get out of Dodge, and fast.

For years, researchers have stated that humans address fear in one of two ways: fight or flight. In either scenario, researchers portray fear as the enemy. I hate to dispel some of this highly esteemed work, but fear does not always have to be the enemy. Your reaction to fear does not have to be either fight or flight. Rather, you can choose to make fear an ally.

Here are some ally qualities:

Unconventional Wisdom

Ignore fear and pay the price.

➤ Fear can be a catalyst.

➤ Fear can be an energizer.

➤ Fear can be a teacher.

➤ Fear can be a focus-enhancer.

Fear Can Be a Catalyst

Fear is a necessary catalyst for change. Fear invites you to ask tough questions, such as:

➤ What is causing the fear?

➤ What is the purpose of this fear?

➤ Is the fear real or imaginary?

➤ How can I use this fear to benefit my life?

The fear can be beneficial, in that it causes us to either reaffirm our current thoughts and actions, or to change. Either of these acts is okay as long as the decision is a conscious one.

Fear Can Be an Energizer

Reflect upon a recent time when you experienced fear. What was going on physiologically? Was your heart beating faster? Did you feel more alert? Were you having an adrenaline rush? All of these reactions point to a higher level of energy. You can use that energy to promote positive change or you can use it to drain you of valuable resources and wear you out. The choice depends on whether you are willing to own the feelings and take control, or whether you are going to relinquish your personal power and surrender control.

Fear Can Be a Teacher

You learn from joy. You learn from sadness. You learn from anger. You can also learn from fear. Fear can be one of the great emotion teachers—but only if you're willing to learn. Let fear teach you which life events scare you. Let fear teach you what your reactions are to these events. Let fear teach you how you normally respond. Then use what you've learned to face fear in a positive way.

Fear Can Be a Focus-Enhancer

It's research time. Go check out five books on public speaking—any five. Turn to the index and look up the word "fear". You will find in every one of these books citations demonstrating that even the greatest of speakers experience some fear every time they speak. The astonishing fact is that they wouldn't trade the fear for anything. Why? They report that when some fear is present they stay on their toes and are sharper and more focused. The fear adds to the professional crispness of their talk. Without fear, their talk would be more complacent and less effective. The fear enables them to show their best. Fear does serve as a focus-enhancer. We can learn from the experience of these speakers. Instead of wishing to be without fear, we can use fear in creative ways in all aspects of our lives.

The Least You Need to Know

➤ Fear can be a friend and a foe.

➤ Control fear, don't let it control you.

➤ Become a student of your own fear.

➤ Use fear to promote positive action.

Part 3
Emotions:
Experiencin' and Expressin'

Sometimes our light goes out but it is blown again into flame by an encounter with another human being. Each of us owes the deepest thanks to those who have rekindled this inner light.

Albert Schweitzer

Love! Everyone talks about it, but so many people lose sight of what it truly means. In this part of your journey you'll reflect on the unconditional aspect of love—love draws us to move past mere infatuation into a deeper connection with others. You can also deepen your connection with all parts of your life when you stop rushing through your day and learn to appreciate each moment for itself. By paying more attention to the present, you'll begin to see how heavily the past can weigh on you, and you'll realize the wisdom of letting go of the past, making a deathbed peace with others, and forgiving yourself.

Chapter 7

Love: That Four-Letter Word

Four-letter words. They're everywhere—on the radio, on TV, on the big screen. Some are words that make a point, others disappoint. Some of them even get "bleeped" (well, they used to get bleeped).

There is one four-letter word that stands above the rest. It is one that should be heralded from the hilltops, shouted from the serpentine streams, and crooned from the craggy canyons. The word at its most simple and complex is *love*.

The word *love* has made its appearance in more songs and poems than any other word. It has been the subject of everything from notes passed among elementary school hands to epitaphs awled on gravestones. It is the most concrete yet elusive of human experiences. Love is the most powerful human phenomenon, yet it is cloaked in mystery.

Love Unconditionally, or Else!

We all have a number of attitudes about love. I'll bet you recognize some of the following:

➤ I'll love you if you buy me that diamond ring.

➤ I'll love you if you get straight A's.

➤ I'll love you if you'll move to the mountains with me.

➤ I'll love you if you sleep with me. (Easy now, this is a G-rated book.)

The "I'll love you ifs..." are demons that diminish relationships. They are the cunning characters of conditional love.

Conditional Love: An Oxymoron Original

Back in the time when Mr. Oxy Moron decided to create a term in his own honor, he was thinking about the state of affairs in his own life. He was reeling from a ragged relationship he thought was based on true love. What he discovered was that it was based on maybes—an informal contract full of "I'll love you ifs...". The true essence of his merger was "looking out for number one" or "what will I get out of this?" Superficiality at its finest. In his disappointment, he coined what became the first oxymoron—"conditional love."

Unconventional Wisdom

If your relationship is based on conditions (I'll love you if...), then heed this warning: Your relationship is in jeopardy. True love can only be unconditional.

Conditional love really is an oxymoron. True love is not conditional. True love is the union of two individuals who foster an environment where both can grow together and individually, where feelings are expressed with a sense of integrity and openness, where mutual concern for the other is present, and where both lives are enriched through the relationship. Love is the ultimate way of growth.

Relationship Sabotage

A conditional-relationship mentality is one characteristic of a relationship in ruin. Unfortunately, it has many partners. Here is a top-10 list of the best ways to sabotage a relationship.

10. Smother the other person (you determine whether that's literal or figurative).

9. Control the relationship.

8. Focus on the Me instead of the We.

7. Don't set mutual life goals.

6. Sacrifice your identity for the other person's gain.

5. Take the other person for granted.

4. Worry only about your own growth.

3. Don't share your value and belief changes.

2. Don't find ways to renew your relationship.

1. Don't allow yourself to be vulnerable.

Reconcile Relationship Realities

Hmm! Relationships are an intriguing aspect of life. Because they are a study in contradictions they produce paradoxical feelings ranging from clarity to confusion, from ecstasy to depression, from being on top of the world to being down in the dumps.

And you thought that this relationship stuff was going to be easy. *Wrong!*

Relationships arouse conflicting feelings in us, and maybe as a result, we have conflicting, even opposing, sayings about what relationships are. How would you go about reconciling the following contradictory statements?

➤ Good relationships just happen.

➤ Maintaining a quality relationship is the hardest work you will ever do.

➤ Miles don't separate true friends.

➤ It's so easy for relationships to wither with distance.

➤ We'll be best friends for ever and ever.

➤ Best friends are like the tide, they come and go.

➤ Love means never having to say you're sorry.

➤ Love means always having to say you're sorry.

➤ I can read you like a book.

➤ I'll never be able to figure you out.

➤ You'll always be the person I married.

➤ You are so different from the person I married.

➤ In effective relationships couples become one.

➤ In effective relationships couples stay individuals.

Action Prompt

Choose one item from the Relationship Sabotage list that reflects something you currently do. Be honest! Now make a commitment to change this behavior by establishing a concrete goal and acting on it.

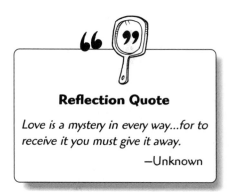

Reflection Quote

Love is a mystery in every way...for to receive it you must give it away.

—Unknown

Power Plate

WENOTME

Reflection Quote

A successful marriage requires falling in love many times, always with the same person.

—Mignon McLaughlin

Whew, that was tough. If you had an easy time reconciling these statements, pick up your relationship therapist license at the door, buy a couch, and hang out your shingle. You're ready to be a therapy guru.

Unfortunately, the reality is that this type of list leaves us frustrated and wondering why we get involved in relationships at all. It would be easy to say "not interested in becoming involved," but that cop-out response would make you miss out on one of the richest parts of life. Let's look at some ways to get a handle on this.

10 Ways to Enhance a Relationship

As you begin to reconcile some of the contradictions of relationships, here are ten things to keep in mind for making them stronger and richer.

10. Strike a balance between holding closely and giving space.
9. Share decision-making.
8. Focus on the we, not me.
7. Make the relationship unconditional.
6. Grow together *and* individually.
5. Never take the other person for granted.
4. Share your goals.
3. Be open about your changing life views.
2. Consciously work on renewing your relationship daily.
1. Strengthen the relationships by allowing yourself to be vulnerable.

Relationship: A Work in Progress

Relationships are the epitome of the evolutionary enterprise. Relationships change from moment to moment and experience to experience. Indeed, it is the change aspects of relationships that make them exciting and fulfilling (even if a little frightening sometimes).

Unconventional Wisdom

Stagnant relationships are not really stagnant—they wither and die.

When you join your life and experiences with another person, you create the unknown, venturing into the worlds of discovery and growth. Your relationship goes through different stages and phases. Your life palette contains the vibrant hues of experience. The picture you paint is up to you. You combine the colors of living to create your masterpiece.

Relationships change. It's a fact of life. They get better or they get worse, but they *never* stay the same. Relationships really are like a roller coaster. Reflect for a moment on relationships you've been in—maybe even the one you're in now. Like the roller coaster, you have your ups and downs, right? So the questions become:

➤ What is the proportion of ups and downs?

➤ Are you happy or unhappy most of the time in your relationship?

➤ What are you doing to increase the ups?

➤ Why are you just letting your relationship be? Do something—*now!*

You change, the person you love changes. You can positively impact your relationship by openly communicating those changes. By sharing, you constantly clarify who you are and what is important to you. You also open the door for the person you love to share. This type of communication prevents the all too common scenario in which one morning, after 15 to 20 years of being together, you roll over in bed, look at your partner, and say, "Who are you?"

Terrific Tension

Give—take. Hold tight—let go. Give freedom—restrict. All these word pairs have a common attribute: tension. I know, when you first hear the word "tension" you think of the negative connotation. Actually, some degree of tension is an essential element for growth. The secret is to discover the optimal amount. Too little tension and there is not enough resistance for growth. Too much and you break. You are the only one who can determine the optimal amount for you.

You have to give and take. You have to hold tightly and let go. You have to give freedom and restrict. Developing the delicate tenor of tension is truly a skill. How do you assess the proper amount? Here are a couple of helpful hints:

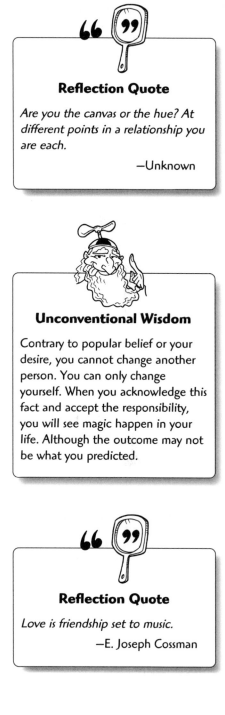

Reflection Quote

Are you the canvas or the hue? At different points in a relationship you are each.

—Unknown

Unconventional Wisdom

Contrary to popular belief or your desire, you cannot change another person. You can only change yourself. When you acknowledge this fact and accept the responsibility, you will see magic happen in your life. Although the outcome may not be what you predicted.

Reflection Quote

Love is friendship set to music.

—E. Joseph Cossman

➤ Occasionally step back and ask yourself, "Self, did I give too much or too little or was there a healthy amount of tension?" This question can be asked of all the word pairs mentioned above.

➤ Ask your significant other, "Did I give too much or too little or was it a healthy amount?"

Hey! That's the same question. At first you might say to yourself, "I can't ask that." But if you are committed to the relationship, if you really want it to work, then you won't even hesitate.

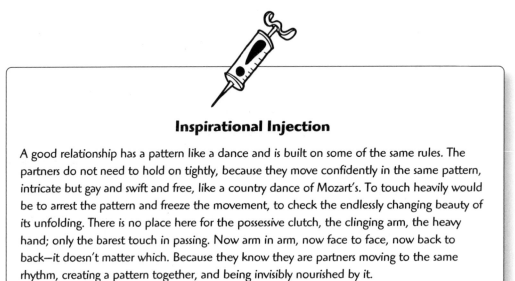

Inspirational Injection

A good relationship has a pattern like a dance and is built on some of the same rules. The partners do not need to hold on tightly, because they move confidently in the same pattern, intricate but gay and swift and free, like a country dance of Mozart's. To touch heavily would be to arrest the pattern and freeze the movement, to check the endlessly changing beauty of its unfolding. There is no place here for the possessive clutch, the clinging arm, the heavy hand; only the barest touch in passing. Now arm in arm, now face to face, now back to back—it doesn't matter which. Because they know they are partners moving to the same rhythm, creating a pattern together, and being invisibly nourished by it.

—Anne Morrow Lindbergh

Moving Past Infatuation

"Did you see her? She's beautiful!"

"He's a hunk!"

"Do you believe how much money he has?"

"She's so powerful and dynamic."

And so the infatuation infection begins. It starts with the tingling sensation created by looks, power, prestige, charm, and material resources.

Being around people with these attributes can be exhilarating. However, these feelings are attributable to mere infatuation, not love. Granted, some relationships that start as infatuation may end up as loving relationships, but infatuation alone cannot sustain a relationship.

Infatuation is the superficial component of a relationship. It might bring two people together initially, but it has no substance. Infatuation has to do with perceptions, not reality.

A strong relationship is based on the character of the people involved. It develops when you allow your personhood to be experienced by another and vice versa. It's based on emotions, values, beliefs, and interests—not on external perceptions.

Have you ever been stricken by the infatuation infection. Are you currently infected?

Intimacy: Nothing Personal

For some reason intimacy has become associated with under-the-covers hot sex (or maybe not so under the covers). These physical connotations of intimacy obscure a much broader view of the concept.

Intimacy is the joining of two souls, whether for a moment or a lifetime. It is measured by an unconditional positive regard and respect for another. It promotes the flow of communication and inspires understanding.

The guardian of intimacy is trust. Trust promotes, sustains, and cultivates intimacy. Although trust is based on reciprocity, don't hesitate to demonstrate your trust first. You will open the door to a fulfilling relationship and foster an environment where intimacy will flourish.

Friendship: An Essential Life Ingredient

When does friendship start? Does it start with the late-night conversation in a dorm? Or drinking a beer after a softball game? Or sitting next to someone in a class, passing notes? Or maybe working on a committee with someone in a church or synagogue?

Action Prompt

Do a little introspection on your current relationship or your most recent one. Is the relationship based on infatuation or true love? Be objective and honest with yourself. Now act on your conclusion.

Reflection Quote

When the satisfaction, security, and development of another person become as significant to you as your own satisfaction, security, and development, love exists.

—Harry Stack Sullivan

Unconventional Wisdom

Your true friends are those with whom you can meet or speak even after a long absence and still have a magic connection, closing the time and distance. You start where you left off just as if moons and miles never separated the two of you. That's true friendship.

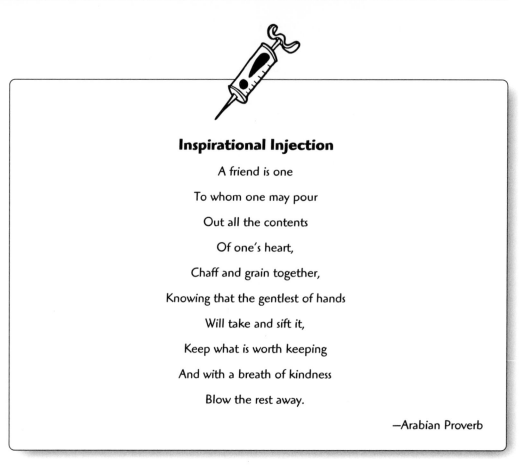

Inspirational Injection

A friend is one

To whom one may pour

Out all the contents

Of one's heart,

Chaff and grain together,

Knowing that the gentlest of hands

Will take and sift it,

Keep what *is* worth keeping

And with a breath of kindness

Blow the rest away.

—Arabian Proverb

Action Prompt

Call, write, or meet with your friend and tell that special person how you feel about him or her. You'll enrich your friend's day and your own as well.

Friendship is a rich ingredient in life's soufflé. It adds the taste, the fulfillment, the texture. But life's soufflé doesn't always turn out well. Sometimes it falls, or parts of it get burned, and sometimes it just tastes stale. Friends help with these disappointments. They provide comfort, the tender hug, or the outstretched hand. Friends let us cry and also help wipe the tears. They strengthen us in times of need.

Friends forgive us when we do stupid things, nourish us when we are emotionally drained, keep us on track when we begin to stray, and speak the truth to us (sometimes even when we don't want to hear it).

1. Who is your best friend?

   _____

   _____

2. What four qualities exemplify him or her?

   a.

   b.

   c.

   d.

3. What do you cherish most about that person?

   _____

   _____

4. What is your favorite memory of your friend?

   _____

   _____

5. How has your life changed because of the relationship?

   _____

   _____

6. What do you do to enhance the relationship?

   _____

   _____

Friends are the people who accept you the way you are. Period. They're always there for you, even when you stumble. They share your joys and sorrows, your ups and downs, your hair color changes and expanding waistline, your defeats, and your accomplishments.

Friendship is a tough but worthwhile job. Get to work!

Power Plate

US4EVR

The Least You Need to Know

➤ Unconditional love is the most powerful love.

➤ Relationship-nurturing is one of the hardest jobs you will ever have.

➤ Intimacy is the connection of souls, not bodies.

➤ Don't pretend that infatuation is love.

➤ Cultivate your friendships; the investment yields great things.

Chapter 8

Slow Down, Seek Wonder, Live Each Moment

> ## In This Chapter
>
> ➤ Is urgency an ally or an enemy?
>
> ➤ What is the last conversation?
>
> ➤ Labor or learning?
>
> ➤ Transitions: Enlighteners?

That's not *just* a flower you walked by. That is a *pelargonium*. It has a petal count, name, unique color specification, and arousing aroma, and it is an attractive playground to several varieties of bugs. But when you walked by, you didn't notice all of that, did you? Your mind might have registered "generic flower," but the urgency in your step prohibited you from *really seeing*. You need to stop and smell the pelargoniums.

Urgency Can Be the Enemy

One enemy we all have in common is urgency. When our lives become so hustle-bustle–oriented we start to lose out on the miracles of living. Of course, all of us pay attention to what are called big miracles—like an eclipse—but the reality is that we miss most of the real miracles of life. We are just too busy to recognize or acknowledge them.

Children can be our teachers in this arena. Have you ever watched a child study a bug? Or witnessed a child blowing soap bubbles, transfixed by the multicolored transparent balloon floating in the air? They *have* the wonder. Urgency is not their enemy. It does not drive them or limit them—that is, not until we get a hold of them.

Power Plate

BALIVE

Reflection Quote

Little minds are interested in the extraordinary, great minds in the commonplace.

—Unknown

Action Prompt

A wise person once said, "How much would you pay to see a sunset if you could only see one in your lifetime?" Don't take another sunset for granted—look today!

To-Now

Bernie Siegel, the esteemed physician and author, shared in one of his lectures the wisdom of a child he was treating who had cancer. The boy said, "We need to live today, tomorrow, to-now." So true. To live to-now is the greatest gift you can give yourself. Enjoying the moment and living in the present creates tremendous tomorrows and fantastic futures. Not living in the now diminishes the moment and the morrow. The choice, once again, is yours.

The Last Conversation

Take a moment and think about the last conversation you had. It might have been as recently as five minutes ago. Did you give the person you were talking to your undivided attention? Did you invest yourself in the conversation? Did you make the most of the interaction?

What would have happened differently if you had treated that conversation as if it were your last? Many years ago I ran across a piece of advice written by a very wise person. It went like this. "Talk with someone as if it is the last time you will ever talk with them." Can you imagine what would happen to the quality of your conversations and relationships if you followed this advice? They would be so much better! You would dispense with the superficial chit-chat and delve into the meaningful dialogue that promotes a relationship.

Your first response to this notion might be: a last conversation is intriguing but not practical. I don't have time to have a last conversation with everyone I talk with.

I'll concede the point, but I'll also suggest that this nugget of wisdom can help you at least look at the tone of your conversations and decide who it's important to have a real conversation with. It's okay to be selfish with your time and energy. So ask yourself how you want to spend your time. Spend your time with people who are positive, people who give you energy (not drain it), who inspire and fulfill you. When you invest your time in these types of people, you want to have real conversations. The "last conversation" idea can be the catalyst to help you prioritize who you will talk to and how.

Reflection Quote

Butterflies count not months but moments, and yet still have time enough.

—The Good Life Almanac

Inspirational Injection

Life is Eternal

I am standing upon the seashore. A ship at my side spreads her white sails to the morning breeze and starts for the blue ocean. She is an object of beauty and strength, and I stand and watch her until at length she hangs like a speck of white cloud just where the sea and sky mingle with each other. Then someone at my side says, "There! She's gone."

Gone where? Gone from my sight—that's all. She is just as large in mast and hull and spar as she was when she left my side, and just as able to bear her load of living freight to the destination. Her diminished size is in me, not her. And just at the moment when someone says, "There! She's gone," other eyes are watching her coming, and other voices are ready to take up the glad shout, "Here she comes!"

—Unknown

Register for a Life Internship

Reflect back to your childhood. Do you remember when adults would come up to you and say, "What do you want to be when you grow up?" Your answer might have been—a teacher, police officer, doctor, lawyer, dancer, fire fighter, president. That was years ago, different dreams and different life views.

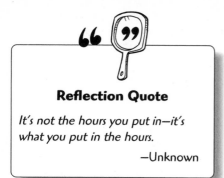

Reflection Quote

It's not the hours you put in—it's what you put in the hours.

—Unknown

Some of us are still trying to figure out what we are going to be when we grow up. The answer is not simple, especially in our rapidly changing society. We no longer get a job and keep it for life. How many jobs have you already had in your life? How many more will you have before retirement? How many will you have after retirement?

The world of work is changing before our very eyes (what *are* "very eyes," anyway?). Not only are our work patterns changing but the nature of the work is changing as well.

Keeping this in mind, I view my jobs as life internships. All jobs have the potential to provide you with additional pieces for your life puzzle. With each new experience come opportunities for growth. Your challenge is to seize the opportunities.

Life is precious, but many folks trudge through it day to day, "putting in their eight" (hours, that is). This type of mentality promotes a more passive view of the world. Just think if you changed the phrase to "creating my eight." Life would start to get richer immediately.

Since life is such a gift, you owe it to yourself to find a job that fulfills your being. I have a test I use to evaluate my job status, and I recommend it to you. Ask yourself these three questions:

1. Am I making a contribution?
2. Am I learning something?
3. Am I having fun?

For me to stay in a job I need to be making a contribution, learning something, and having fun. If one of those is missing, then it's time for me to look for a new job.

Here is another way to look at it, for you math types. It can be put into a multiplication formula:

$$\text{Making a contribution} \times \text{learning} \times \text{having fun} = \text{job fulfilment}$$

This is a multiplication formula because if any one of the factors is 0, then the product is 0. It takes all three factors to make a enriching job.

Preparation Next

There are no dead-end jobs. In fact, each job serves as a new signpost on your journey. I can safely say that you will never have a job that isn't worthwhile in some way. Now don't equate worthwhile with positive. Many times our greatest learning experiences are not positive or are not lessons from positive role models. We might learn which jobs we don't want to do or which behaviors we don't want to emulate, for example. Regardless of the kind of job, however, that job helps us clarify our values, beliefs, and desires. We also learn skills and develop talents. The person you are today is a combination of different pieces of your life. Assembled, they make *you!*

Let's see how this fits with your current job.

1. My current job is as a .... (can be a homemaker, student, unemployed adventure seeker, lawyer, etc.):

   _____

   _____

2. One of the greatest skills I have learned from the job is:

   _____

   _____

3. One thing I've been exposed to in this job that I definitely don't want to emulate is:

   _____

   _____

4. Other experiences that prepared me for this job were:

   _____

   _____

5. This job is preparing me for:

   _____

   _____

6. Three ways I can look at this job as a life internship are:

   ➤ _____

   ➤ _____

   ➤ _____

Unconventional Wisdom

Life internships prepare you for other life internships which prepare you for other life internships. Graduation day is when your mission on earth is finished.

Reflection Quote

I always knew that I would look back on the bad times and laugh but I never knew I would look back on the good times and cry.

—Unknown

Wake Up to the Internship

Your alarm rings, signaling the beginning of a new day. The sun is perched at the horizon with its morning greeting. You wipe the sleep from your eyes and your mind turns to the future, the events of the day. After a shower (whether you needed it or not), some breakfast, and a quick perusal of the paper, you head off to work— or let me rephrase that: You head off to class. Yes, class! That's what work really is. It's a classroom rich with opportunities for learning.

Work really can be viewed from the student perspective. It is an internship. You learn about:

➤ Skills

➤ Work-place dynamics

➤ Yourself

➤ Other people

➤ The industry

➤ How an organization relates to the larger society

➤ Taxes (aargh!)

➤ Interpersonal relations

➤ Responsibility, accountability, and all the other abilities.

Wow! This learning stuff can be exhausting. You didn't realize that you could learn that much from a job, did you?

Change the Mind Set

By changing the mindset from "I'm going to labor" to "I'm going to learn," you invite opportunities for growth. Your day is more exciting and more fulfilling. When you talk with successful people, you quickly find that they embrace the learning mind set. They surround themselves with books, experiences, and teachers that will facilitate and foster their learning. Successful folks have an unquenchable thirst for learning. They also say that the more they learn, the more they want to learn. It is a perpetual cycle that increases in magnitude as life goes on.

Hey, try this. As you're coming home from work each day, challenge yourself to identify one thing you learned from the day. Do this for a two-week period. I encourage you to write down the lessons. After you have 10 learnings written, you might want to try another week. Pretty soon, it will be part of your life. You will look forward to recounting the day. In fact, you'll find that you make deliberate attempts to enrich the day so that you'll feel good about the lessons you write.

Let's practice with today.

One thing I learned at work today was:

_____

_____

_____

Great! You're already one-tenth done with your first two-week period.

One other tidbit that helps in this process is to begin your day by telling yourself to be on the lookout for learning possibilities. Ask yourself this question: "What lessons can I discover today that will help me be better than I was yesterday?" You'll be amazed at how this awareness mentality will provide you with abundant gifts for growth.

Transitions: The Great Mystery

Imagine this scenario. You're hiking along a root- and rock-riddled path lined with lush vegetation. You see a collection of sun streams filtering their way to the forest floor through the canopy of leaves overhead. A boulder up ahead grabs your eye. You see a snakeskin molded against the hard surface of the stone, creating a beautiful contrast in texture. Its brittle translucent structure looks hand-painted, with intricate patterns. The skin was left behind as the snake began another phase of its life.

Are you ever like the snake? Do you ever shed one skin and create another? Sure! We all do. Life is a series of transitions from birth to death, transitions revolving around:

➤ Career choices and changes

➤ Dynamic family structures

➤ Relocations to new communities

➤ Values and beliefs

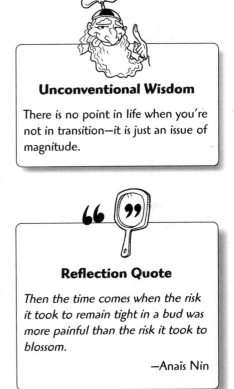

Unconventional Wisdom

There is no point in life when you're not in transition—it is just an issue of magnitude.

Reflection Quote

Then the time comes when the risk it took to remain tight in a bud was more painful than the risk it took to blossom.

—Anaïs Nin

The Ultimate Bridge

Transitions can serve as the bridge from ignorance to enlightenment, but you have to be willing to cross over to discover the riches. Sounds simple enough, doesn't it? But do you ever just look at the negative side of a transition, seeing just the chasm and not the bridge? If you are like most of us, you don't want to surrender your security. (If you're not like most of us, you can skip to the next section—but first be sure that you don't have something to learn from this.)

Explore for Enlightenment

I'm glad to see that you stayed with us for this section. It will be worthwhile for you, because I want to pass along a story shared by Sheldon Kopp, a noted author and therapist. It goes like this:

> Enlightenment and the freedom it brings are always imminent, but our very efforts to catch hold of what we are seeking may prevent us from discovering what is already there. There is the image of the man who imagines himself to be a prisoner in a cell. He stands at one end of this small, dark, barren room, on his toes, with arms stretched upward, hands grasping for support onto a small, barred window, the room's only apparent source of light. If he holds on tight, straining toward the window, turning his head just so, he can see a bit of bright sunlight barely visible between the uppermost bars. This light is his only hope. He will not risk losing it, and so he continues to strain toward that bit of light, holding tightly to the bars. So committed in his effort not to lose sight of that glimmer of life-giving light, that it never occurs to him to let go and explore the darkness of the rest of the cell. So it is that he never discovers that the door at the other end of the cell is open, that he is free. He has always been free to walk out into the brightness of the day, if only he would let go.

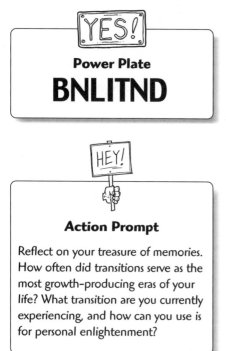

Power Plate

BNLITND

Action Prompt

Reflect on your treasure of memories. How often did transitions serve as the most growth-producing eras of your life? What transition are you currently experiencing, and how can you use is for personal enlightenment?

Kopp's story offers some incredible insights worth heeding. Enlightenment is available to you, and especially during transition periods, you need to let go of the bars and explore the darkness of the cell. During transitions you probably want to hold onto the bars more tightly, to strain to see that little light of hope, but to ignore the rest of world is to deny yourself growth. As you search about the cell called "transition," listen to your inner voices and strive to answer the questions that they pose. Although the answers may seem elusive, the process enables you to create pieces of self which will fit into the larger mosaic of your life. During transitions, you learn a great deal about yourself, you refine your thinking, and you mold your character. Although the process may be emotionally draining, you will definitely reap the rewards!

Positive Perspectives

Transitions are not easy, especially since emotions are involved. However, your approach to dealing with them will dictate what you learn and the intensity of the emotions aroused. A positive mind set will help you greatly during these times. There are two types of transitions: those you choose and those you don't. Profound, huh?

Many transitions in your life you ask for, such as marriage, births, a new house, career, and college. When you usher these events into your life, you can anticipate more effectively the challenges they present. By anticipating, you can prepare and use tools to help you cope with these life changes. And when you form a union between anticipation and a positive mindset, you cultivate a climate for positive growth.

Although you ask for many transitions, there are many you do not and would not choose—layoffs, job transfers, family deaths, illness. These are much more difficult to deal with since you don't have the luxury of anticipation. Your choice now becomes how to view the life change as an opportunity rather than a setback. By making the conscious decision to grow from the experience, you accelerate the process and learn from it more quickly.

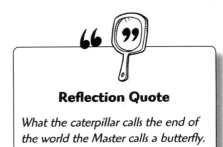

Reflection Quote

What the caterpillar calls the end of the world the Master calls a butterfly.

—Richard Bach

Transitions can serve you in a very important way—they can be a pivotal link between mediocrity and greatness. They can propel you to a greater understanding of life and enhance your resiliency.

The Least You Need to Know

➤ Stop and enjoy the moment.

➤ Make work a life internship.

➤ Make your talk meaningful.

➤ Transition yourself for growth.

Finish Unfinished Business

In This Chapter

➤ Why do you need to tell 'em how you feel?

➤ Do you really bury the hatchet?

➤ How do you finish the unfinished?

➤ Forgive: to do it or not?

There is one aspect of living where good intentions are simply not good enough: letting others know how you feel. You need to transform those intentions into action. If you don't share with others how you feel about them, then many things can result:

➤ You lose out on opportunities for relationship enhancement.

➤ You keep the lines of communication guarded.

➤ You might never get a second chance.

This last one is the kicker. What would happen if you didn't get a second chance? Two people would lose out—you and the other person.

Inspirational Injection

Compassion is being in tune with oneself, the other person, and the whole world. It is goodness at its most intuitive and unreflective. It is harmony which opens itself and permits the flowing out of love towards others without asking any reward. It avoids using people as tools. It sees them as complete and without a need to be changed.

—David Brandon

Let 'Em Know How You Feel

You also might become a victim of the guilt-complex virus. Guilt is one of the sicknesses that looks for any avenue into your body. Once it finds its way in, it spreads. And like many viruses, it can stay in the body for a lifetime, rearing its ugly head from time to time.

The most effective way to deal with the guilt virus is to get it before it attacks you. Prevention is paramount. It can be as simple as letting another person know how you feel. At first, this might be somewhat difficult and awkward, but with practice it becomes a normal part of living.

Now I'm not talking about fancy anniversary dinners, or holiday gift-giving, or sending birthday cards—although these are important. I'm talking about day-in and day-out messages that connect you to the other person. This continual confirmation and communication keeps the relationship renewed, rejuvenated, and rewarding. It provides an immediacy that offers real feelings, just in time.

Here are some benefits of "telling them how you feel":

➤ You connect soul to soul.

➤ Both parties are enriched.

➤ There will be no unfinished business.

➤ You create a whole relationship.

➤ You free yourself by not harboring ill feelings.

Interpersonal Insights

"I never knew you felt that way."

"Why did we take so long to tell each other how we felt?"

"My life is different now because of what you said."

By disclosing your feelings, you let your true personhood shine through. You penetrate into deeper levels of a relationship and discover greater treasures.

There is a caveat, though. When we talk about sharing feelings, we paddle uncertain waters. Whether you are telling people how much they mean to you or that they have disappointed you, you must realize that the response may not be what you expected. They may need time to reflect upon your words, to feel what you said. Initially, they may not be ready to hear what you said. Whatever the case, be prepared to listen. You also may want to think a little about how to share the information, so that it will be most meaningful and accepted by the other person. But don't think so much or for so long that you never get around to doing it!

Deathbed Peace—No Regrets

She stares at the sterile white walls, feeling the sheets covering her frail body. She can hear the machines that have worked in concert with her body but that will no longer serve her as she prepares for her hour of death. As she reflects on her life, a warm peace fills her being. She has no regrets. She let the significant folks in her life know how she felt. She didn't leave behind any unfinished business. She reflects and rejoices in her past. Serenity envelopes her, and as her breathing stops her new life begins.

Is your life at peace? Could you be on your deathbed tomorrow, rejoicing at your past and eagerly looking to your future? Have you finished your business?

Unconventional Wisdom

Sharing feelings creates authentic relationships that sustain us during difficult times, enhance our joys, and strengthen our hearts.

Action Prompt

Today, not tomorrow, make a phone call, pay a visit, or write a letter to deal with some of your unfinished business. Use this occasion to tell someone:

"Thank you for making a difference in my life."

"You are very important to me."

"I'm sorry, please forgive me."

"I forgive you."

Do it now, before it's too late.

Inspirational Injection

They were brother priests and brother Jesuits. They had for many years experienced a rich and rewarding friendship. The two had trudged together through the wilderness of the long seminary training. When one had a special need—for time, a listening ear, or whatever, the other had always been there.

The friendship was ended abruptly in tragedy and death. One of the two friends was hit by a car and killed in front of the residence where the two priests lived with their community.

When the other was informed that his friend lay dead on the street, he went running through the cordon of onlookers and police, and knelt at the side of his old friend. He gently cradled the dead man's head on his arm , and before all those gaping people, he blurted out:

"Don't die! You can't die! I never told you I loved you."

—John Powell

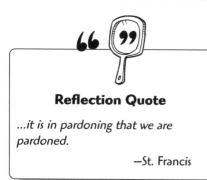

Reflection Quote

...it is in pardoning that we are pardoned.

—St. Francis

Bury the Hatchet

Recently I was riding in my S.U.V. (Super ultra-testoster-one vehicle) listening to music when a Garth Brooks tune came on and this line dripped from his lips: "We bury the hatchet but leave the handle sticking out."

Hmm. It is hard to bury the hatchet, isn't it? We say, "no problem, I forgive you." Then, when times get tough, we resurrect the hurts from the past. The hatchet is swinging again.

I could get rhetorical on you and pose questions that don't require answers, but I've decided to get pragmatic and offer some questions that you get to answer.

1. Why is granting forgiveness so hard?

_____

_____

2. What keeps you from forgiving?

_____

_____

3. When you *do* forgive, how do you feel?

_____

_____

4. When you harbor ill feelings and don't forgive, how do you feel?

_____

_____

Okay, let's get a little more personal.

1. Identify a person you have not forgiven for something and what that something is.

_____

_____

2. What is stopping you from forgiving that person?

_____

_____

3. What are you gaining by not forgiving that person?

_____

_____

4. Is it worth the price?

_____

_____

5. What is one step you can take toward offering this person forgiveness?

_____

_____

Reflection Quote

Forgive them, for they know not what they do.

—Jesus

Unconventional Wisdom

Life is short and we never have enough time for gladdening the hearts of those who travel the way with us. Oh be swift to love! Make haste to be kind.

—Henri Frederic Amiel

"I'll never forgive her."

"What he did is unforgivable."

"Forgive? Forget that!"

"I'll never speak to him again as long as I live."

"She committed the unpardonable sin."

Have these words ever spewed from your mouth? Okay, so maybe not these exact words, but how about the sentiment? It's hard to think about forgiving someone when they've hurt us, wronged us, or betrayed us.

I was talking with a student of mine about her family. She told me that her father and uncle had not spoken to one another for 30 years. When I asked her why, she said that they couldn't even remember what the fight was about.

What a shame! The sad part is that there are a lot of relationships like that out there. You might even be in one. I challenge you to move beyond such barriers to forgiveness as pride, stubbornness, and the need to control.

Withholding forgiveness creates a negative force that diminishes your sensibility and limits your self-actualization. Forgiveness cleanses the soul. It restores positive energy that propels you into the world of possibilities, opportunities, and optimal living. When you choose to forgive, you choose to live—*fully!*

Benefits of Forgiving Others

The benefits of forgiving others are too numerous to list, but here are a few. See if you can think of a few of your own.

➤ Releases negative emotional energy

➤ Brings closure to the event

➤ Serves as a healing agent

Power Plate

I 4 GIV U

➤ Allows you to give to the other person

➤ Gives the other person another chance

➤ Enables you to show another side of yourself

➤ Enables you to serve as a role model for others

➤ Creates a better society

➤ Gives you peace of mind

Forgiveness: The Big Ask

Making a mistake is easy. Asking for forgiveness is hard. In fact, for some it is very hard.

Asking for genuine forgiveness has two essential components:

➤ Ask.

➤ Change the behavior.

You can't repeat the mistake. When you ask for forgiveness but then repeat the offending action, you erode your credibility and your words ring hollow. Ask, really mean it, and grow.

Forgive Thyself

Who are you going to spend the most time with in your life? *Yourself!* Now that we've established that, consider this: have you ever made a mistake? Of course you have (never mind the old joke: "I once made a mistake. That was the time I thought I made a mistake but I was wrong"). How often do you forgive yourself when you make a mistake? What happens if you don't forgive yourself and carry those feelings around with you? Basically, they fester and you end up a miserable mess. You negatively impact your life and the interactions you have with others.

Self-forgiveness is hard to do. For some of us, it is almost impossible. We can be our own worst critic, we can beat up on ourselves, we can punish ourselves—sometimes we are harder on ourselves than anyone else could be.

We've already discussed the importance of forgiving others. It is just as important to forgive yourself. Forgiving yourself also requires behavior change on your part. You are making a commitment to yourself to grow.

Reflection Quote

The measure of an individual's real character is what that person does when he or she knows that no one else will find out.

—MacSalay

Reflection Quote

Learn to forgive yourself again and again and again.

—Sheldon Kopp

Reflection Quote

Have patience with all things, but first of all with yourself.

—St. Francis de Sales

1. Identify something in your life for which you have not forgiven yourself.

_____

_____

2. What are you gaining by not forgiving yourself?

   _____

   _____

3. What are you losing out on in life because you won't forgive yourself?

   _____

   _____

4. What do you think would happen if you did forgive yourself?

   _____

   _____

5. What is the first step you can take on the road to forgiving yourself?

   _____

   _____

The Least You Need to Know

➤ Tell 'em how you feel—*now!*

➤ Bury the hatchet.

➤ Finish your business. Have no regrets.

➤ Forgive yourself. It's an essential part of life.

Part 4
Service: Help Others and Help Thyself

You give but little when you give of your possessions. It is when you give of yourself that you truly give.

Kahlil Gibran

Service—it sounds so noble (and boring), but in fact it can be one of life's greatest joys. Once you start to practice it, you'll do it, not out of altruism, but because it nourishes your soul in a way that nothing else does. To begin the life of service, you'll learn to stop fixating on yourself and discover what talents and abilities you have to offer—no matter who you are or how busy you are, you can make a difference. And once you, like others, learn the great joy of service, the individual hours of service you give will become transformed into a life of service.

Chapter 10

Force Yourself to Volunteer. Say What?

In This Chapter

➤ Volunteerism: Why is it a must?

➤ Bellybuttonitis: Do you have it?

➤ How to ditch the TV remote

➤ Quality of life: Where does it come from?

"Force yourself to volunteer." What kind of chapter title is that? It just doesn't sound right. Let me explain. I require all of my students to volunteer in a human service agency of their choice. They have to do it because it is part of their grade (that is called *incentive*). I "force" them. Of course, they always want to have a discussion about the incongruity between the words *force* and *volunteer*. It's always an interesting discussion.

Force...Persuasion

Here's my view. If you look at the research conducted by the volunteer experts, you'll find that only about one-fifth of those who currently volunteer do so on their own accord. The rest were forced somehow—no, not with a gun to their heads but by more subtle means: through affiliation with service organizations, churches and synagogues, human service organization boards, and yes, even classes.

Most people who volunteer did not wake up one day and say, "Yes, today is the day I'm going to volunteer!" For those of you who were internally motivated in this way, we applaud you and commend your spirit. But the majority of people did not do it that way.

Reflection Quote

There never was a person who did anything worth doing who did not receive more than he gave.

—Henry Ward Beecher

Back to my students for a moment. When they hear that there is a volunteer requirement—a mere 10 hours for the entire semester—they groan and clamor that they don't have time. They also don't see how it relates to class. But something incredible happens between the distribution of the syllabus on the first day of class and the handing-in of evaluations on the last day of class. Consistently, the evaluations state that this was one of the most powerful experiences they have ever had.

An interesting aspect of volunteering is that once you do it, forced or not, you get hooked. It transforms your life and makes you look at the world in a different way.

Inspirational Injection

From the mouths of those who were *forced* to volunteer—my students:

"Even though at first I hated being forced to do community service, I know now that I would have never done it, had it not been 'forced.' You cannot always learn life's lessons within your comfort zones."

"I believe volunteering exercises one's emotional muscle. There is a sense of wholeness added to one's life when volunteering. It also puts life in perspective and lets me appreciate what I have."

"From volunteering I have learned the nobility of serving others."

"When I left my volunteer site every Monday, I always felt satisfied that I had made a difference in people's lives. I *knew* they had made a difference in my life."

"To volunteer is to give a piece of yourself away and get hundreds of pieces in return."

"I learned through volunteering that life can grow through the ashes of our tragedies."

Bellybuttonitis: It's Epidemic

Many years ago I heard a friend accusing another friend of having *bellybuttonitis*. When I heard the term my ears perked up (they didn't actually move) and I had to smile.

Bellybuttonitis. What a great term. I don't know who coined it—obviously someone much wiser than I am—but that person provided us with a great metaphor for a syndrome that permeates our society.

Let's look at the term a little more closely. Bellybuttonitis. In its simplest form it means that the world revolves around your bellybutton. Your needs, your desires, your wants are all that matter in this world, right? (I'll let you down easy.) Probably *not!*

Bellybuttonitis is a syndrome that definitely needs to be reckoned with. So take your eyes off your belly so that we can get started.

The causes of Bellybuttonitis are:

➤ Sense of personal urgency

➤ Societal pressures to succeed, evidenced by pursuit of big titles and bank accounts

➤ Having many more wants than actual needs

➤ The ubiquitous mandate to look out for #1

➤ The feeling that if you look out for someone else, you will somehow lose out

Power Plate

HLPSOM1

The personal symptoms of bellybuttonitis include:

➤ Sore neck from looking down at one's torso so much

➤ Lack of close relationships

➤ Mediocre success because you place limits on yourself

➤ Loss of learning, since you're missing out on learning opportunities outside your realm

The organizational symptoms of bellybuttonitis are that:

➤ The organization does not get full use of your gifts and talents.

➤ Collaboration is stifled.

➤ Stress is exacerbated, which affects morale and productivity.

➤You become too cautious, thus inhibiting growth.

So we've looked at causes and symptoms of this syndrome. Where do we go from here?

First of all, why don't you take a little inventory?

1. Are you ever a victim of bellybuttonitis?

_____

_____

2. What situations prompt this syndrome?

   _____

   _____

3. What role does urgency play in your particular case?

   _____

   _____

4. What relationship is there between your confidence level and bellybuttonitis?

   _____

   _____

5. What are three things you can do to break out of the bellybuttonitis pattern?

   A. _____

   B. _____

   C. _____

One of the easiest ways to escape the bellybuttonitis plague is through service—helping others. Is that on your list of three? If not, add it and make it your fourth method.

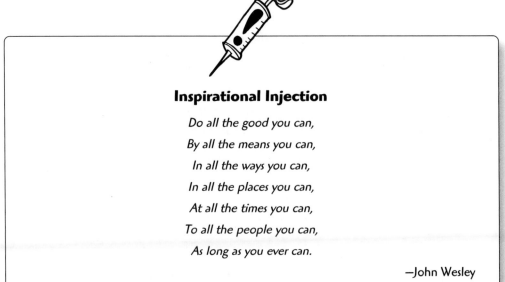

Inspirational Injection

Do all the good you can,

By all the means you can,

In all the ways you can,

In all the places you can,

At all the times you can,

To all the people you can,

As long as you ever can.

—John Wesley

Exercise Service: Put Down the TV Remote, Stand Up, and Reach Out

Think back to yesteryear, before high-resolution TVs and CD players; before fiber-optic communication and computer chip technology; before silent movies and Victrolas. It was a time characterized by a slower pace, strong work ethic, and solid community values. You helped your neighbors raise a barn or mend a fence, and you provided for them when they were ill. During that era folks were outside *with* others, not inside insulated *from* others.

Whether it's the TV or the CD player or the hectic work week—it's time to say "enough is enough." Stand up and reach out. You are an integral part of the community.

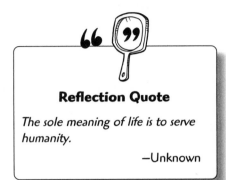

Reflection Quote

The sole meaning of life is to serve humanity.

—Unknown

Put Down the TV Remote

How much television do you watch? Five hours a week? 10 hours? 40 hours? The bottom line is...a lot! What do you think would happen if you invested just one hour of your TV time each week to service—to helping someone else? In the course of a month, you would have touched another life for four hours; in half a year, 26 hours; and in one year, 52 hours. By giving of yourself just one hour a week, you can make an indelible imprint on the lives of other people. Let's try something.

Start with Monday and write down the TV shows you watch and their respective times (include the news).

Weekly TV Viewing

Program	Time	Number of Hours
Monday		
1.		
2.		
3.		
4.		
5.		
	Total hours _____	

continues

continued

Program	Time	Number of Hours
Tuesday		
1.		
2.		
3.		
4.		
5.		
		Total hours _____
Wednesday		
1.		
2.		
3.		
4.		
5.		
		Total hours _____
Thursday		
1.		
2.		
3.		
4.		
5.		
		Total hours _____
Friday		
1.		
2.		
3.		
4.		
5.		
		Total hours _____
Saturday		
1.		
2.		
3.		
4.		
5.		
		Total hours _____

Program	Time	Number of Hours
Sunday		
1.		
2.		
3.		
4.		
5.		
	Total hours _____	
	Grand total hours _____	

Add up the total number of hours you watch TV each week. Now for the math. Divide the total number of hours by 168 (the number of hours in a week) and you have the proportion of time you would be devoting to serving others each week. You can afford that, can't you?

So go back to your list and identify one hour per week that you are willing to give up. (I know that some of you skipped this activity because you really didn't want to know the answer. It doesn't matter. You got the point.)

Stand Up

Now that you've identified your hour, stand up and go look in the mirror. Ask yourself, "What do I really believe in and how could I help someone else?"

This stand-up routine is very important, because you will be much more likely to continue with volunteer service if it is associated with something you are passionate about.

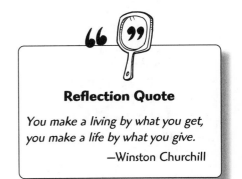

Reflection Quote

You make a living by what you get, you make a life by what you give.

—Winston Churchill

Reach Out

Okay. You've identified your hour, you've found something you are passionate about, and now you have to *act*. You have to actually go out and serve.

Service is not writing a check; service is face-to-face, person-to-person, heart-to-heart, and soul-to-soul. It might take a while to get to the soul-to-soul part, but many times in volunteering relationships, you get there faster than you think. But don't look at soul-to-soul as a threat; look at it as an opportunity. Besides, most of the time it comes naturally.

Now your exercise is complete!

Do Time: In the Community, That Is

Do you know what distinguishes one community from another?

A. The number of fast-food restaurants

B. The timing of the stop lights

C. The pet leash rules

D. The quality of life

...and your answer is _____ .

Yes—D. You're right again. Do you ever get tired of always being right? Sorry, that's another topic.

Quality of life personifies the uniqueness of community. Of course, the goal for any community is a high quality of life characterized by good schools, cultural opportunities, low crime, low teen-age pregnancy rates, low unemployment, and health care. Quite an extensive array of attributes, but nonetheless an optimal living environment for all of us.

To help you get a handle on what makes a quality community, I'll first tell you what it is not:

Power Plate

LIV2SRV

Reflection Quote

Benevolence is community. There can be no community without involvement and no involvement without vulnerability and no vulnerability without risk.

—M. Scott Peck

➤ It is not federal, state, and local government mandates.

➤ It is not bricks and mortar.

➤ It is not physical location.

Rather, quality of life is people serving people. A high quality of life is a direct product of people working together toward common goals. And it's not formal organizations with paid employees that make the difference. Our society's transformations have come from those individuals who have devoted their time and energy to serving others, usually without pay.

Volunteers have come to the forefront in helping with natural disasters, serving on school boards, advancing human rights, and touching lives in health and human service causes.

We all need to "do time" in the community. Although you may initially see doing time as restrictive or as a sacrifice, the reality is that it is liberating and fulfilling. You become part of something bigger and better, creating an environment in which the members can flourish.

You won't be given a number, a striped suit, or a ball and chain—you'll be given exciting challenges and opportunities that you can mold into a quality way of life.

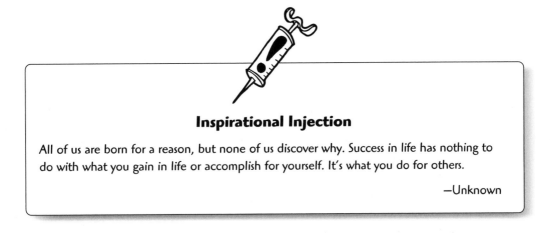

Inspirational Injection

All of us are born for a reason, but none of us discover why. Success in life has nothing to do with what you gain in life or accomplish for yourself. It's what you do for others.

—Unknown

Brainwashing Is Okay

I believe in brainwashing, especially when it comes to helping others. Every day when my two daughters go out the door for school, I tell them two things: "I love you," and "help someone out today." My hope is that by hearing those words a thousand times, they will internalize them. My dream is that 10, 20, or 30 years from now my girls will hear a voice in their head when they open the door to begin their daily routine. Of course, what I want them to hear is "I love you—and help someone out today"! Brainwashing really can be a good thing when the message is positive. Feel free to use it on yourself and others.

The Least You Need to Know

➤ Your bellybutton will be fine; look out for someone else.

➤ Trade an hour of TV for an hour of service.

➤ Reach out and touch a life.

➤ The community needs you.

Chapter 11

Give an Ounce, Get a Pound

In This Chapter

➤ What really is generosity?

➤ How do you create a miracle?

➤ What are the benefits of service?

➤ What are the gifts you have to give?

Many years ago, I was at my parents' house. It was my daughter Katie's birthday and she was talking with Mrs. R., her grandparent's neighbor. Mrs. R. had lost her husband to Alzheimer's disease a year earlier, which left her financially strapped and very lonely. As Katie talked with Mrs. R., you could see the magic in the elderly woman's eyes. In the course of the conversation, young Katie told Mrs. R. that it was her seventh birthday. The woman and Katie had a splendid conversation about birthdays, with Mrs. R. sharing recollections from her past. After the exchange, Katie ran back out into the yard to play. Several hours later, there was a knock at the door. At the entrance stood Mrs. R., wearing a frayed dress and over-worn shoes. She had in her hands a gift—a birthday present for Katie. Mrs. R. gave Katie one of the most precious presents she would ever receive, for in the bundle tied with a wrinkled ribbon were a box of raisins, a used set of crayons, and a dollar bill.

Generosity at Its Finest

Generosity! That present brought a lot of joy to a little girl. That gesture of the human spirit helps us understand what generosity really means.

Plant a Seed, Grow a Miracle

Imagine yourself in a small rural village in China. A local farmer explains to you that seeds were planted in this field five years ago. He urges you to bend down so that you can notice the plants beginning to break through the soil. A grin travels across his stoic, weathered face. You are about to take a six-week trek throughout Asia and this is your first stop. You bid the farmer farewell and agree to come back and visit him at the end of your tour.

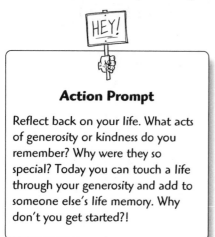

Action Prompt

Reflect back on your life. What acts of generosity or kindness do you remember? Why were they so special? Today you can touch a life through your generosity and add to someone else's life memory. Why don't you get started?!

Six weeks later you return to the small village. When the farmer sees you in the distance, he goes to you and says, "I have something special to show you." He takes you to the field where you had seen the plants breaking ground after five years of apparent inactivity. To your amazement, the landscape has been transformed. You are awestruck as you gaze at the field that was vacant a mere six weeks ago. Now it is filled with ninety-foot (yes, 90-foot) Moso bamboo trees. While you were gone they were growing about two and one-half feet a day! You could literally watch them grow.

Here is a plant that displayed no growth for five years, yet gigantuan growth in the period of a few months. For years the Moso bamboo tree has served as the great metaphor for planting seeds. How does this fit in with serving others? When you give of yourself to another person, you are planting seeds. Some of the seeds you plant will bear fruit immediately, but others may not come to fruition for years. At some point, when the conditions are just right, the evidence of previously planted seeds will come to the surface. When this happens, the person will think back and say, "Now I understand what she was teaching me years ago" or "I've never needed the skill he taught me years ago—until today—and it made all the difference."

When you invest yourself in the life of another, sharing your riches—yourself—you can have an impact on that person for many years to come. In fact, you may change a life forever.

Interconnectedness: Harness People Voltage

A colleague shared with me an illuminating activity that illustrates the power of interconnectedness. The first thing you need to do is to go to one of those nature and science stores that have hatched in America's malls, where you can buy a special gadget. It looks like a Ping Pong ball, except that it has two metal pieces on the exterior. Here's how it works. You assemble a group of people in a circle and ask them to hold hands. You're also in the circle. In one hand, instead of holding another hand, you are holding the special ball. You put your finger on one of the metal pieces and the person next to you touches the other metal piece (don't worry, you won't get shocked). When the connection is made and the circle is complete, the ball lights up and music is generated. Keeping your finger on the metal piece, and your neighbor likewise, you ask someone in the circle to let go of a hand. When that person does so, what do you think happens? You're right—the connection is broken; the music stops and the light goes out. When you ask them to hold hands again, the light goes back on and the music plays again.

It takes the complete connection to make the ball work. When the connection is broken, the ball just will not work.

This activity serves as a great metaphor for life. What happens when you really connect with someone?

➤ Energy surges through your body.

➤ Your interest in life gets elevated.

➤ You feel a natural high.

➤ Your excitement for the present is enhanced.

These things and a lot more really happen. Connecting person-to-person is one of the most powerful aspects of life we can experience.

There is a way to intensify the experience even more. That is to connect with someone who is different from you—a person who walks a different path in life.

Power Plate
NTRKNKT

Unconventional Wisdom

When you volunteer, who are you really helping?

Power Plate
NRGIZE

I'll give you an example. I, along with two colleagues, had the opportunity to take 15 college students to Honduras. Our goal was to go to a mountain village to help the villagers—to teach them about good health behaviors. Honduras is the poorest country in Central America. Neither I nor my students had ever seen poverty like that. Our eyes were opened, the strings of our hearts were pulled, and an unforgettable imprint was made on our souls. It didn't take long to connect, despite language barriers. Our purpose was to help enrich their lives, but we were the ones who left enriched.

When you move out of your comfort zones, especially your cultural comfort zones, you see the world with different eyes. I want to emphasize, though, that you do not need to go to another country to experience another culture. You can do it in your own hometown.

Here are some questions for you to ponder:

1. When was the last time you helped someone?

   _____

   _____

2. Was that person from another culture?

   _____

   _____

3. What prompted you to help?

   _____

   _____

4. What service opportunity could you pursue in your community that would involve you with a different culture from your own?

   _____

   _____

5. What's keeping you from getting involved?

   _____

   _____

6. How might you make a difference by becoming involved?

   _____

   _____

7. Are you willing to challenge yourself to try it? Why? Or why not?

   _____

   _____

8. Do you need a gentle nudge? Consider yourself so nudged. When will you start?

   _____

   _____

Interconnections increase our power—our personal power, our professional power, and our societal power. When we unite our energies, our limitations dissolve and we position ourselves for success and fulfillment. You directly determine the voltage in your life. Plug in *now!*

In Their Own Words

Let's hear more words from the mouths of those who have done it—volunteer, that is. These are important lessons we can learn from those who shared their precious time with others:

Action Prompt

Commit to four hours of helping someone in another cultural realm. You only have to count to four. Make it something that is face-to-face, and then evaluate the impact it has had on your life. Start this week—don't put it off.

"It seems as if sometimes when I volunteered, a different me came out. I would end up talking about things such as God and the importance of living life to its fullest. These are not subjects I usually get into conversations with people about. But I realized that I have a lot of insightful things to say about these types of subjects."

"If you take an hour or two out of your week, you give a gift that keeps giving."

"I went into this experience thinking that I would be bringing something into other people's lives. Instead I feel that I walked away with something more. The people I visited provided me with laughter and filled my heart with joy."

"The reinforcements of volunteering are natural rather than materialistic."

"Volunteering gives me a feeling of self-worth and can be seen as a method of 'repaying' the people of my community for enabling me to lead a life free of hardships, while providing me with the security that help will be provided if I'm ever in need."

"Volunteering showed me that the limitations of life are only created by my own desire and that through the growth of my heart, the 'I' can grow as a complete person."

"To give much is to receive much more."

"Through volunteering I learned that I have to do more than just think good thoughts, wish for peace, and want good things for people. I learned that I *have to act.*"

"It was humbling to think that just by listening I made a difference."

"If volunteerism is an outpour of the heart, we will meet the challenge to live in a manner to outlove, outbless, and outserve."

"Volunteering is fun and fulfilling. I made a commitment to share my time, my knowledge, my laughter, my hugs, my smile, and myself. It's good to know when you are doing something right."

"I have not only learned to count my blessings but how important it is to share them."

"Volunteering helped me come out of my fog of ignorance."

"Volunteering made me realize how much I have to offer others. I may not have a lot of money to give, but the simple gift of time, effort, and affection can go a long way."

Reflection Quote

God does not work in all hearts alike, but according to the preparation and sensitivity he finds in each.

—Meister Eckhart

Unconventional Wisdom

The greatest gift you can give someone else is you.

Life Gifts: Open and Share

Often when I tell my students that they have to volunteer, the response I receive from them is, "How can I volunteer? I don't have anything to give?" I really like when they give me this answer, because it provides me with the opportunity to tell them how wrong they are—in fact, they have everything to give.

I ask them:

➤ Do you have a hand? Good. It can be used to hold someone else's.

➤ Do you have ears? Good. They can be used to listen to someone's story.

➤ Do you have a heart? Good. It can be used to warm another's.

➤ Do you have feet? Good. They can be used to walk part of life with another.

The gifts you have are many, the opportunities you have to share them are ubiquitous, and the impact you'll make is profound. Don't ever sell yourself short. The gifts are there waiting to be opened and shared.

Assess Your TSAs (Talents, Skills, and Abilities)

You have special talents, skills, and abilities that combine to create the unique mosaic of an incredible person. Yes, you are incredible. Sometimes you don't give yourself the value you richly deserve. It is your uniqueness that makes you a miracle.

Let's delve deeper in identifying your gifts.

1. What are three things you do well?

    a.

    b.

    c.

2. How can you use these to touch another person's life?

   a.

   b.

   c.

3. Choose one of the things you do well and create a realistic goal statement that you can strive to accomplish.

_____

_____

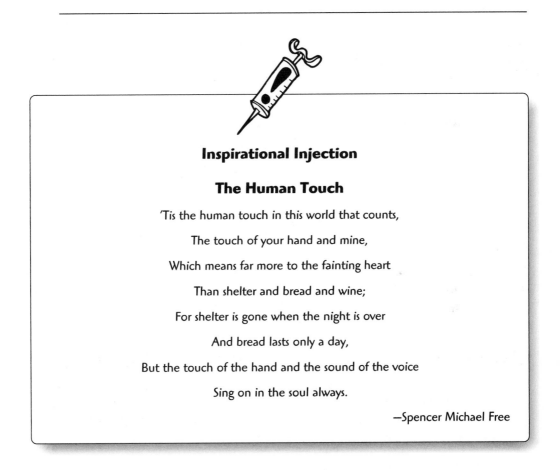

Inspirational Injection

The Human Touch

'Tis the human touch in this world that counts,

The touch of your hand and mine,

Which means far more to the fainting heart

Than shelter and bread and wine;

For shelter is gone when the night is over

And bread lasts only a day,

But the touch of the hand and the sound of the voice

Sing on in the soul always.

—Spencer Michael Free

The Gift of Comfort

When I was a child, my Dad used to say "when you volunteer, you give the gift of comfort, and when you comfort someone you strengthen them." I've never forgotten that.

111

Think back to a time when you were lonely or depressed; or maybe a time when you were ill; or maybe a time when you were in need...and someone comforted you. Do you remember that magic feeling? That feeling of being strengthened. That feeling of "Yes, I can make it through another day."

When you give of your talents, skills, and abilities—when you give of *yourself*—you strengthen, you comfort, you make a difference.

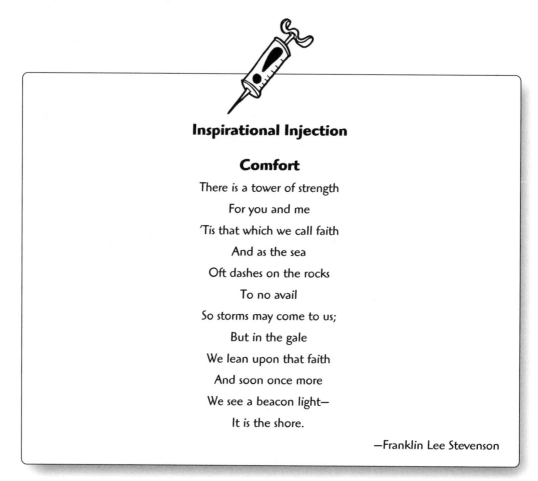

Inspirational Injection

Comfort

There is a tower of strength

For you and me

'Tis that which we call faith

And as the sea

Oft dashes on the rocks

To no avail

So storms may come to us;

But in the gale

We lean upon that faith

And soon once more

We see a beacon light—

It is the shore.

—Franklin Lee Stevenson

"Service Is Love Put Into Gear"

One day I was traveling the rural roads of Virginia and passed a small white clapboard country church. I noticed the sign announcing the upcoming sermon: "Service is love put into gear." What a great title for a sermon! What a great dictum for life. When your actions are motivated by love, you touch people at a different level—you approach their souls. This is the essence of *authentic giving*—giving that is unconditional, unselfish, and unencumbered. Through authentic giving, you move past the superficialities of day-to-day living and enter the world of moment-to-moment miracles.

Day of Caring—Life of Caring

Once a year in my community the local United Way sponsors an event called "A Day of Caring." Area businesses allow their employees to take the day off to help others less fortunate than themselves. These folks shed their suits and hosiery and don work clothes and gloves. They become an army of workers wielding paint brushes, hammers, shovels, and big hearts.

Hundreds of volunteers give a day of their lives to serve others. It is a powerful day. The magic of the day does not end with the sunset. The needy were helped and the helpers were needed. For many of those served and those who were serving, the day provides a catalyst for a Life of Giving.

Power Plate

GIV2LIV

Giving: A Compound Investment

Investments 101

Simple Investment Goal	To get a return greater than the amount you originally paid
Compound Investment Goal	To get a return exponentially greater than what you originally paid

The term *exponentially* is the key indicator of the difference between simple and compound investments. That's financialese.

In terms of volunteerese, there is no such thing as a simple investment. When you give of yourself you always make a compound investment because you are giving from a uniquely whole person. You can't give just part of yourself. The return is compounded and worth much more to the recipient and to you than the original cost of the action.

Simply put: When you give, the returns are substantial and life-changing. This is compound investing at its finest.

The Least You Need to Know

➤ Real generosity is giving from the soul.

➤ You can make miracles every day by touching lives.

➤ The return on your giving investment is many times greater than you might imagine.

➤ You have the gifts to give. Use them.

Chapter 12

Heart Gifts

In This Chapter

➤ What can we learn from water?

➤ What is a "stewardshipper"?

➤ What's all the talk about heartstrings?

➤ What is the ultimate libation?

Years ago, when my interests were playing Kick the Can and shooting hoops with my male friends (and girls were just a nuisance), a significant event happened that I will always remember. The city where I lived had just been inundated by a major flood. The flood disrupted the water system and so potable water became scarce. An emergency mandate was issued stating that water would be rationed until the crisis was over.

I remember my Dad asking us in his booming voice, "Hey kids, do you want to go with me to have some fun? They need help at the fire department giving out water to people." I went along with a couple of my brothers and sisters. Mom stayed home so that she could taxi the other kids who had prior commitments. As we were leaving the house, I know Mom smiled and told us something like, "Be cheerful givers."

Unconventional Wisdom

I looked in my dictionary for the word *water*. To my amazement I discovered that following the initial entry of the word, there were 239 compound words with water as the lead word. Hmm. The power of water in our lives is evidenced yet again.

Reflection Quote

The best and most beautiful things in the world cannot be seen, nor touched...but are felt in the heart.

—Helen Keller

Unconventional Wisdom

The greatest good we can do for others is not to share our riches with them, but to reveal theirs.

—Unknown

When we arrived at the fire house there was a line of folks waiting to get their water rations. Serving them was a cadre of volunteers. As a volunteer I remember getting to wear a cool white armband with a large red cross on it. It was a little too big for me, but I proudly wore it, grinning from ear to ear.

When our turn to serve came, I stood next to my Dad, watching for direction and feeling his supportive guidance. We poured a lot of water that night, including our own ration. When we got home, Dad thanked us for going. He was right—it had been a lot of fun.

Water Lessons

Years later as I reflect on that experience, I realize that my Dad was a teacher that day (as he was for us every day). He was teaching us how to serve others, but he did so in the way he always has—through his example. He didn't preach, although he certainly could have, since he's an Episcopal priest and excels in the pulpit. He didn't say, "Here are the lessons you should have learned from this." He just served, with us by his side. Little did we know that he was intentionally planting seeds for the future.

The lessons I learned from that day have been many. But the most powerful can be described poignantly by the act we were performing. We were giving water—the sustainer of life.

Normally, if I wanted to teach you the lessons of serving others, I would just take you along with me so I could teach by example. But since we can't do that, I'll have to share some of the lessons the next best way—through words on a page. Here are several examples.

➤ Be a cheerful giver.

➤ Giving can be fun.

➤ Be a role model for family, friends, colleagues—and for those you don't even know are watching.

➤ Serve your neighbors.

➤ Watch, learn, serve, watch, feel, serve.

Stewardshipper Extraordinaire

I'll bet you didn't know that one of the most powerful positions in the world is really an avocation: Stewardshipper Extraordinaire. You won't see this title on any business card or organizational chart. Usually you won't even know that someone is a Stewardshipper Extraordinaire until your life has been touched by him or her. The work is done quietly, sometimes planned, sometimes spontaneously. These folks are often like the Lone Ranger—you turn around to thank them and they are already gone. (They don't wear masks, though. Masks are prohibited by Federal Law 4U2.B-SRVR.#1.)

The position of Stewardshipper Extraordinaire has four job components: to serve, to protect, to nurture, to challenge.

A person does not need to perform all of these roles with one individual to receive distinguished Stewardshipper status; however, doing so is not uncommon. Let's look at these roles a little more closely:

➤ **To Serve:** This one is pretty straightforward. You are doing something to help others meet their needs. You provide some type of service—a helping hand, a listening ear, or an inspirational insight.

➤ **To Protect:** Don't get nervous. You don't have to carry a gun. Protection comes in a variety of forms. It can be as simple as sharing a lesson you learned from a mistake you made, so that the other person won't make the same mistake. It can also be providing an objective voice or sharing a different perspective. The trick is learning how to walk the fine line between protection and overprotection.

➤ **To Nurture:** This role focuses on support: being there when the person needs you, providing a shoulder to cry on, praising their accomplishments, giving them a hug of acceptance.

➤ **To Challenge:** Nudge them to move beyond their comfort zone. Help them to clarify their values. Assist them with learning from their mistakes. Encourage them to grow and extend various aspects of their personhood.

Reflection Quote

I shall pass through this world but once. If therefore, there be any kindness I can show, or any good I can do, let me do it now; let me not defer it or neglect it, for I shall not pass this way again.

—Grellett

Whew! This Stewardshipper Extraordinaire business sounds like some tough stuff. Sure, at times it *is* tough—but if it weren't, you wouldn't be Extraordinaire, would you?

You might assume that to be a Stewardshipper Extraordinaire, you'd have to have a long, close relationship with a person. Certainly, to perform some of these roles some element of trust must have been established; however, much stewardshipper work is done with total strangers.

Power Plate

BKIND

Examples abound, from investing a Saturday to work with someone participating in the Special Olympics program, to helping a lost child find her Mom in the megastore, to letting the person behind you in the grocery store check-out line go in front of you since she has one item and you have 52.

Here is a real-life example. My oldest brother travels the Capitol Beltway in Washington, DC every day. This paved thoroughfare is like a mountain river, at times rushing at great speeds and at other times still and stagnant. The driver is at its mercy.

The beltway banality doesn't affect my brother, though. He has the patience of Job and a gigantic heart. He's always on the lookout for someone who needs help. One day he happened upon a man who was standing next to a vintage dented car (not to be confused with a fine immaculate antique). The vehicle was precariously jacked up on this dangerous road.

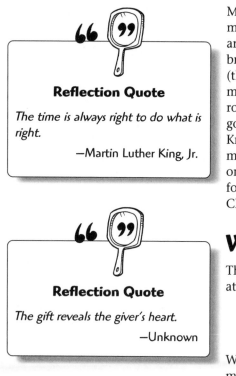

Reflection Quote

The time is always right to do what is right.

—Martin Luther King, Jr.

My brother stopped to see how he could be of help. The man had removed the blown tire from the rustmobile and the man needed to get it to a tire fixer-upper. My brother told the man that he would get the tire fixed (there was no spare—I hate when that happens). When my brother got to the nearest gas station and began rolling the flat, worn-out tire, he realized that even if he got the tire repaired, a new flat was in the making. Knowing that the owner of the worn tire had very little money, my brother decided that a new tire was in order—so he bought one. Christmas came a little early for the man who had been stranded. But for my brother, Christmas comes everyday.

Reflection Quote

The gift reveals the giver's heart.

—Unknown

With Strings Attached

The favorite refrain of many a deal maker is "No strings attached." Well, today I want to offer a new mantra:

With strings attached—*heartstrings,* that is!

When deeds are tied with heartstrings, they become much more precious and meaningful. All true acts of serving another have heartstrings attached. That's what true giving is all about. The giving is not done because of a sense of obligation, shoulds or oughts—it's authentic. True giving is a gift from the heart.

The Ultimate Libation

You stand behind the bar listening to the woes and lamentations of folks glued to the bar like barnacles to a ship. You are not an ordinary bartender, though. You have been enlightened. Your life experiences have taught you the recipe for the ultimate libation.

The music drones in the background as the patrons' flirtatious eyes dance back and forth trying to secure some shared moments. As you work behind the bar, you wait patiently for "the question." Finally you hear it. With resounding clarity it bellows above the cacophony of sounds and is music to your ears. A person new to the bar asks, "What is the best drink someone can get around here?" You pause, and then slowly, with your Zenlike look, say, "Ahh—that would be 'Kind Spirits.' It's the drink of life." The person on the barstool glances at you as though you have totally lost your mind, but he's intrigued enough to hear you out.

"Kind Spirits," you say, "is full and robust. It's made of the following ingredients."

Your patron, patronizing you, says, "Is this going to take long or do I need to go ahead and order something else?" You reply that it will only take a minute—a Montana minute, however, not a New York minute.

You continue. "Kind Spirits is made of:

>3 parts self-confidence

>2 parts soul

>Garnished with a slice of humility"

You've got the patron interested. He bites and says, "Okay, tell me what the parts of the mixture are."

You continue.

>*Self-Confidence*

Part 1: Eliminate the word "cannot" from your vocabulary.

>Challenge yourself to learn.

>Set yourself up for success.

Part 2: Practice new skills.

>Expose yourself to new experiences.

>Get the most from on-the-job training.

Part 3: Affirm your abilities.

Give yourself permission to make mistakes.

Create a support network.

Soul

Part 1: Offer your true self to another.

Part 2: Practice what you believe.

Humility

A slice of humility adds the ingredient that keeps self-confidence from becoming arrogance.

Unconventional Wisdom

The richness of your life can be measured by the quality of your service.

—Robin Sharma

Power Plate

HRTGFTS

Your patron listens, then replies, "Hmm, I didn't realize that I would get a life lesson today. I think I'll order one of those 'Kind Spirits.' And how about a nice cold beer to go along with it? Thanks."

Too Busy to Serve

Too busy to serve. Help! This is not a good thing. When you are too busy to serve, you are too busy to live fully. That's the truth. When we don't have time to serve others, we occupy the confining space called egocentricity. We erroneously believe that the world revolves around us. Doubtful!

Human beings are interdependent creatures. We rely on others to complement our shortcomings, teach us new things, and help broaden our horizons. Others depend on us for these functions as well.

You can give someone else something that no one else can give them—*you*. Yes, treasures from your own personal stash of experiences, knowledge, skills, and feelings.

Here is the prescription for Too-Busy-to-Serve Syndrome:

Rx:

Look for someone in need.

Help with only heartstrings attached.

Give of your essence.

Make serving others part of your routine.

Recommend this prescription to others.

Promote the service concept through your example.

Repeat daily.

Inspirational Injection

College Spring Break. The time of the great exodus to the sand, the sea, and the sunburn. Party time! This has been the ritual for years. A week of pure self-indulgence. Let me give you a glimpse of another type of spring break. It's called Alternative Spring Break. In 1998, about 120 James Madison University students trekked to places like the Nature Conservancy in Florida and planted over 20,000 trees. Others went to the Johnson Brinson Center in Florida to work with at-risk youth. Some traveled to Louisiana to work in an AIDS community, while another group traversed the roads of Appalachia to build a home. In all, about 17 sites were visited. Bikinis, swim suits, and beers were replaced by work boots, hammers, ice cold water...and the spirit of giving. The single goal of the excursions was to serve others. Let their example become our example...and let their actions become the honored tradition.

Serving others is a privilege and a responsibility. The nobility of service is one of the greatest treasures of the land. Serve. Live. Thrive. Enjoy.

The Least You Need to Know

➤ Give the gift of life.

➤ Tie all your acts with heartstrings.

➤ Become a Stewardshipper Extraordinaire.

➤ Enjoy the libation of life.

Part 5
Pespective: Get It

Look to this day
for it is life, the very life of life.
On its brief course lie all
the verities and realities of your existence;
the bliss of growth, the glory of action,
the splendor of beauty.

For yesterday is but a dream
and tomorrow is only a vision,
but today well lived makes
every yesterday a dream of
happiness and every tomorrow
a vision of hope.
Look well, therefore, to this day
Such is the salutation of the dawn.

—Sanskrit 1200 BC

In the concerns that fill our day, we can lose sight of the big picture and what matters most. We need to regain perspective. As you reflect on the lessons in this part of the book, you'll learn to start finding the humor in life again. You'll also be able to see life's obstacles for what they are: opportunities. And in your relations with others, you'll come to understand in a richer way the importance of the community—not the one you happen to find yourself in, but the one you make.

Chapter 13

Tame the Roller Coaster

In This Chapter

➤ Taming life's roller coaster is a must

➤ It could be worse

➤ Straightforward strategies for keeping perspective

➤ Welcome obstacle opportunities

Viper, Grizzly, Iron Wolf, Raptor, Loch Ness Monster—what do all these names have in common? You guessed it, they're names of famous roller coasters around the country. The names are supposed to evoke a sense of dread and fear—and they thoroughly thrill those who dare to ride them.

Although you may be one who chooses to seek thrills with these twisting, turning, thrusting, plummeting metal monsters, you know that in two and a half minutes the ride will be over, and you can go back to normal. Unfortunately, your life sometimes feels like a big roller coaster, and instead of knowing that the gyrations will stop momentarily, you feel totally out of control.

Your challenge is to tame the roller coaster of life. You need to look at the external and internal influences and seek understanding. Understanding is the key to being a great tamer, and taming is the key to creating a proper perspective.

Roller Coasting: Making Sense of the Ups and Downs

Reflect back to a time when you were on a roller coaster. Imagine the fearful clackity-clack of the car on the tracks as it inches its way up the steep incline. Nervous laughter fills you as you near the top; then you peek over. The raucous ride begins. You suddenly plunge straight down, only to be jerked sharply into a curve, drop again, then start upward. For a brief moment of peace and sanity, you try to get more comfortable and catch your breath (and anything else you have lost on the ride). Your peace is abruptly disturbed by the return of the clackity-clack sound and the realization that another plunge is near. When the ride finally ends and your white knuckles return to their original shade, you laugh like a school child, and then quickly adjust your hair (those of you who have hair).

Action Prompt

Identify one thing you worry about over which you have no control. Now, discard it and worry about things over which you do have control.

The ride was fun, and you might even do it again. Nothing like getting your heart beating fast and enjoying a thrill.

Aren't our lives a lot like a roller coaster? We have ups and downs, unexpected turns, feelings of calm and exhilaration. Yet (if you are like the rest of us in this world) these feelings sometimes turn into a sense of being overwhelmed. When was the last time you were overwhelmed? Last year, last month, yesterday, today, now? Those of you who chose "last year," choose again—and tell the truth this time.

Here is a multiple-choice question for you. What happens when you feel overwhelmed?

A. You become less effective.

B. You become less patient.

C. You become accident-prone.

D. You become irritable.

E. You lose perspective.

F. All the above.

And the answer is...F, of course. In fact, there are also a lot of other things that happen to us.

Let's go back to our roller coaster car analogy (this time we'll choose a middle seat). The highs and lows in life challenge you and make you grow; if life is nothing but extremes, however, the equilibrium of your existence is negatively affected. You lose your perspective. So you need to have a more consistent, less radical ride.

Inspirational Injection

We who lived in the concentration camps can remember the men who walked through the huts comforting others, giving away their last piece of bread. They may have been few in number, but they offer sufficient proof that everything can be taken from a man but one thing: The last of his freedoms—to choose one's attitude in any given set of circumstances, to choose one's own way.

—Victor Frankl

Human beings are creatures that need equilibrium (all of you non-human beings reading this can skip to the next chapter). Your equilibrium comes from a sense of balance and control. The key is to enjoy the highs, learn from the lows, and buffer both extremes with a strong foundation of consistent, maintained being. You can create a more subtle roller coaster ride and in turn promote a healthier perspective on life.

Equilibrium in life is not, however, a product of haphazard good fortune. It takes work—*diligent* work. You must take deliberate steps to enhance your own existence.

Dear Mom and Dad, Please Sit Down Before You Read This

One of the steps we need to take toward positive perspective is an examination of self as it relates to the outside world. Our first simple step is to decide what is *really* important.

Let's look at this idea from a different angle, from the words of the ubiquitous copy-machine letter. You know the kind of letter I am talking about. Someone in your office or school gets this anonymous copy-machine letter. They like it and give you a copy. You like it and march directly to the copy machine to make copies for your friends. (Of course, you have to wait in line behind all of the other people who are making copies of this letter for *their* friends.) This type of letter is really the grown-up version of the chain letter. We just circumvent the post office.

Here is a letter that has been passed around the bastions of the academy for years. Like a holiday fruitcake, the same one exchanges hands many times.

Dear Mom and Dad,

It has now been three months since I left for college. I have been remiss about writing and I am very sorry for my thoughtlessness in not having written before, but I will bring you up to date now. But before you read on, please sit down. Do not read any further unless you are sitting down. Okay?

I'm getting along pretty well now. The skull fracture and concussion I got when I jumped out the window of my dormitory when it caught fire is pretty well healed. I only spent two weeks in the hospital. Now I see almost normally and get the sick headaches only once a day.

Fortunately, the fire in the dormitory was witnessed by a gas station attendant, and he was the one who called the fire department and ambulance. He also visited me in the hospital. Since I had nowhere to live because of the burnt dormitory, he was kind enough to let me share his apartment with him. It's only a basement room, but it's kind of cute. He is a very fine boy, and we've fallen deeply in love and...plan to get married. We haven't set the exact date yet, but it will be before my pregnancy begins to show.

Yes, Mother and Dad, I'm pregnant. I know how much you are looking forward to being grandparents. I know you will welcome the baby and give it the same love, care, and devotion you gave me when I was a child.

The reason we are delaying our marriage is that my boyfriend has a minor infection which prevented him from passing the premarital blood test. I carelessly caught it from him, but this will soon clear up with the penicillin injections that I am taking daily. He is kind, and although not well-educated, he is ambitious.

Now that I have brought you up to date, I want to tell you that there was *not* a dormitory fire, I did not have a concussion or skull fracture, I was not in the hospital, I am not pregnant, I am not engaged, and I do not have a venereal disease; however,...I *am* getting a D in history and an F in science, and I wanted you to keep it in the proper perspective.

Love, Your Daughter

Perspective—it sure is a product of how we look at things. It's also different for each of us.

AAA Perspective-Protection Plan

We all want to succeed. We want to be safe. We want life to be wonderful. But oftentimes we do little to ensure this state of living. The key to keeping life in perspective and enhancing our own personhood is to take advantage of the AAA Perspective-Protection Plan. This plan is tried, true, and terrific.

Awareness

Do you ever notice butterflies in your stomach? How about that thousand-pound weight you sometimes carry on your shoulders? Or maybe you find yourself heaving a heavy sigh? These are all feelings that contribute to your perspective, or lack thereof.

It's time to act like a car mechanic. As the mechanic does with a car, you need to listen to the pangs, sounds, whirs, and vibrations that come from your body. The body serves as a great perspective barometer, if you'll only listen to it—and you can do this without getting grease under your nails.

One of the keys to enhancing awareness is to make a commitment to being aware. Sounds simple doesn't it? Well, you know as well as I do that it is not. Some people can't make a commitment, even when their life depends upon it. Of course, that is not you—so we can move on. Self-awareness takes work and attention. But by making a commitment you have taken your most important step—the first one.

Reflection Quote

I used to worry about having no shoes to walk the street, until I met a man who had no feet.

—Unknown

Power Plate

OPN YRii

Inspirational Injection

If the earth's history could be compressed into a single year, the first eight months would be completely without life, the next two would see only the most primitive creatures, mammals wouldn't appear until the second week in December, and no homo sapiens until 11:45 on December 31. The entire period of man's written history would occupy the final 60 seconds before midnight.

—Richard Carrington

In addition to listening to your body, listen to the voices in your world. Being aware of the outside voices allows you to put your life in a different context. It allows you to become part of the bigger picture. If you listen only to your own voice and become totally absorbed in your own world, then you're just like an individual puzzle piece—not knowing how or where you fit.

Anticipation

Reflect for a moment on the times that you've been a little out of sorts, maybe on edge or when you've blown one more issue out of total human proportion. You know, one of those times when the loss of perspective got the best of you. What precipitated these little emotional blips?

Power Plate

The big question to ask yourself is: *Could I have anticipated this?* (Is that big enough?) Anticipation plays an important role in the perspective-maintenance process. In fact, much of what you lose your perspective over can be traced directly back to something that could indeed have been anticipated. And the great part about this is that it doesn't take a stellar sleuth to discover the event.

Pull out your pen and list those events or activities facing you that you *can* anticipate might push your perspective pulse out of whack:

_____

_____

_____

_____

_____

This step is critical in the perspective-enhancement process. When you combine the awareness piece of the plan with the anticipation piece, then you are ready for the next piece: action.

Action

Lights! Camera! Action! *Life Perspective*—the movie of your life, starring *you*. You prepared yourself for this part by first becoming aware, then anticipating. Now you are ready to act. Here's a tough question for you: Do you ever get right up to the point of taking action, but then for some reason you don't follow through? No, you would never do that, would you? Well, maybe sometimes.

When you don't take action, you waste the precious time you invested in becoming aware and anticipating. If you are not willing to take action, then by all means don't take the other two steps. But I have a secret for you. Come closer so that I can whisper to you: If you don't become aware, if you don't anticipate, if you don't take action, then there is only one person who will lose out—you. You owe it to yourself to employ the power of perspective in your life.

Action means doing things, taking concrete steps that will help you maintain perspective. List below some things you do now, consciously, to keep life in perspective. Then list some others you could start today—and do them!

Action Prompt

Take 15 minutes today to listen to one of your favorite albums, eight-tracks, tapes, or CDs from your younger days. Enjoy the memories.

Current Things I Do:

_____

_____

_____

_____

_____

Additional Things I Will Do:

_____

_____

_____

_____

_____

Unconventional Wisdom

There is nothing new under the sun...except for everything.

Reflection Quote

Obstacles are what you see when you take your eyes off of the goal.

—E. Joseph Cossman

Unconventional Wisdom

During the 1997 World Series, a game was being played in Cleveland, with snow coming down and a 20° wind-chill factor. One of the team managers, after hearing numerous complaints about the cold from players, finally had heard enough. He got them all together and said, "Would you rather be with the other 26 teams at home in front of the fire, or be here playing in the World Series?"

Prepare for Ornery Obstacles

I want to share with you something I learned from the consultant world, which is just northeast of Jupiter. This is one of the tools of the trade that has been floating in the universe for some time now. Like jokes, consultant learning activities travel like wildfire throughout the consulting community, being modified as they make their journey. Usually the originator of the activity is unknown—and this one is no exception. Having said all that, here it is—a life tool for you.

This part of the chapter requires active participation. This means you—yes, *you*, the one holding the book. Ready? Okay. Place the book where you can see it and in such a way that you will have one hand free. Now make a fist with your free hand, and put it in front of your face. Then raise only your index finger from the fist. Your finger should be straight ahead in front of your eyes. Now, focus on your finger. It's a fine finger, isn't it? Now, keeping your finger there, look past your finger and focus on something beyond it. Even though you are focusing on something beyond your finger, you can still see your whole finger, right?

Okay, okay. I'll tell you where we are going with this, but first put your finger down and assume your normal reading position.

Your finger represents an obstacle. The focal point beyond your finger represents a goal. Too often what happens is that all focus goes to the obstacle—in this case, the finger. When you do this you in effect paralyze yourself and impede positive action. If all focus stays on the obstacle, then you lose sight of your goal and perspective.

What you need to do is to focus on your goal (even if you need to don your trifocals). By focusing on your goal, you can get through and past the obstacle—and you'll be able to put it in its proper perspective.

Inspirational Injection

The Oyster

There once was an oyster whose story I tell

Who found that sand had got under his shell;

Just one little grain, but it gave him much pain,

For oysters have feelings although they're so plain.

Now, did he berate the working of fate

Which had led him to such a deplorable state?

Did he curse out the Government, call for an election?

No; as he lay on the shelf, he said to himself,

"If I cannot remove it, I'll try to improve it."

So the years rolled by as the years always do,

And he came to his ultimate destiny—stew.

And this small grain of sand which had bothered him so,

Was a beautiful pearl, all richly aglow.

Now this tale has a moral—for isn't it grand

What an oyster can do with a morsel of sand?

What couldn't we do if we'd only begin

With all of things that get under our skin?

—Author unknown

Don't Be a Woeful Wannabe

Wannabes—they are everywhere. It's easy to be a Wannabe, because it doesn't require any commitment or work.

➤ Wanna enhance your self-esteem?

➤ Wanna create proper perspective?

➤ Wanna enjoy life more?

Then leave your Wannabe status behind and *become!*

133

Taking on Obstacles

When you're ready to leave Wannabe behind, become an obstacle remover. Here are a few suggestions how.

➤ Use the anticipation skills you just learned. Remove obstacles before they actually become obstacles by being proactive.

➤ Keep the big picture in sight. See how the obstacles really fit into the big scheme of things.

➤ Annihilate annoying nuisances that are insignificant but present themselves as legitimate obstacles. Invest your time in dealing with real obstacles, not impostors.

At the same time, explore how to become an Obstacle Opportunist.

➤ Appreciate the gifts obstacles show you. They force you to look at life in a different way, thus enhancing your perspective and your existence.

➤ Use obstacles to tap into and develop dormant parts of yourself. Also use these opportunities to expand your network of individuals who can help you grow.

➤ See the obstacle as a challenge, not as a threat. Challenges excite and ignite, threats irritate and debilitate.

Now, third, practice being an Obstacle Realist.

➤ Some obstacles we face are events or activities over which we have no control. Acknowledge them, stop worrying about them, and move on!

➤ Recognize that obstacles are a part of life. You will never eliminate them, nor do you want to.

➤ Some obstacles are mere inconveniences, while others are serious threats. Know the difference and act accordingly.

Unconventional Wisdom

Total absence of problems would be the beginning of death for a society or an individual. We aren't constructed to live in that kind of world. We are problem solvers by nature, problem-seekers, problem requirers.

—John W. Gardner

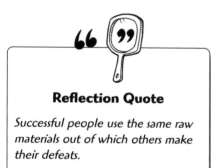

Reflection Quote

Successful people use the same raw materials out of which others make their defeats.

—Bernie Siegel

The Least You Need to Know

➤ Roller coasters are a part of life—make the most of them.

➤ Perspective protection is up to you.

➤ Determine what is really important in your life.

➤ Use obstacles optimally—they can be gifts.

Chapter 14

Laugh, Seriously!

In This Chapter

➤ Learn how to prospect for laughs

➤ Complete your PHI (Personal Humor Inventory)

➤ Discover why you should laugh at yourself

➤ Get the humor prescription for health

Let's try something. Look at what page you're on so you don't lose your place. Now turn to the opening letter on the inside front cover of the book. You'll need to indulge me for a moment. I need you to count the number of *e*'s you see in the letter. I'll wait while you count. (You can imagine that there is some elevator music in the background while you count.)

OK. Finished counting? How many *e*'s did you find? I'll bet you had no idea that there were that many *e*'s in the letter. I know when you first read the letter, you didn't say to yourself, "Wow, there sure are a lot of *e*'s in this letter." Why didn't you say that? Because you didn't notice them, and you didn't notice them because you were not looking for them. You found them when you were specifically looking for them. Seek and ye shall find.

Seek and Ye Shall Find

Pretty powerful phrase, huh? I would guess so…it's from the Bible. Do you think that Matthew had humor in mind when he quoted Jesus? I don't think so, but I'll bet both would probably agree that it applies to humor as well: when you seek it, you will find it.

Become a Humor Prospector

Now is your opportunity to add a new job title to your resume: Humor Prospector. You can be an explorer, a discoverer of the precious life gem called humor. This will probably be the easiest prospectin' you've ever done. You won't get dirty and you don't even have to use picks, shovels, or pans. In fact, the humor gem is so plentiful that you will need to use a totally different set of tools to find it.

Prospecting Tools

Here are some of the tools you'll need.

Selective-Perception Geiger Counter. Your brain is an incredible tool. Although at first glance it just looks like a convoluted mass of gray clay, its intricacies and capabilities are profound. One portion of your brain has a selective-perception Geiger counter in it. This prospecting instrument enables you to program an object or phenomenon that you want to lock onto if it comes anywhere within your perception field.

You've all experienced this. For example, you go out and buy a new car, the only one like it you've ever seen. The day after you buy your new car, you notice that everywhere you look, you see a car like yours. Yikes, how can that be? Well, before you bought the car, your Geiger counter was not programmed. Once you bought it, the program was set.

So let's get to work. Get inside your brain and turn the selective-perception Geiger counter to the Humor position. Turn it on, and you are ready to go. You will now see humor everywhere because you are making a conscious decision to discover it.

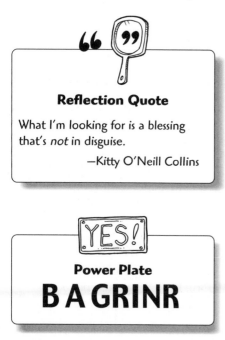

Reflection Quote

What I'm looking for is a blessing that's *not* in disguise.

—Kitty O'Neill Collins

Power Plate

YES!
B A GRINR

Humor Voyeur Prospecting Glasses. First of all, I need to make something clear. Humor voyeur prospecting glasses are *not* for looking into people's private lives. This pastime has gained such notoriety in our society that we now have TV shows entertaining millions through funny videos taken in yards, living rooms, and parks throughout the nation. But these glasses are designed to help you see the humor of people in everyday life.

Whether you are at work, at home, in the airport, or on the subway, when you put on your prospecting glasses you will see the lighter side of people. I'll give you one example. My seven-year-old niece was with her grandfather bailing out water from a flooded basement. After doing this for quite a while, she paused in the middle of her bailing, turned to her grandfather and said, "I feel like Cinderella; at this rate I will never get to the Ball!" Children can be great humor teachers.

Comics Cache-Ometer. This prospecting tool enables you to find intentional humor every single day, and is quite simple to use. It's located at the tip of your fingers. All you have to do is to open your daily newspaper, turn to the back, and you've discovered one more vein…the comics of funny papers. Yes, someone wrote those comics to provide you with some humor. Comics give your day a good perspective start. I've always wondered, though, why they usually precede the classified ads. Is it to help those looking for jobs to keep a sense of humor about the whole affair?

Humor Maps. Reflect for a moment on the route you take to work, school, or the grocery store. If you're like most people, you take the same route almost every time. Your initial discovery of that terrain is a faint memory. What happens if you change your map and use a different route? Immediately, new discoveries are revealed and new riches can be harvested.

So it is with humor. You need to expand your humor maps. Don't look for it only in the places you've found it in the past. Explore different mines called literature, movies, plays, music, and malls. You will find that there are rich lodes in these mines waiting to be discovered. Open your eyes to new terrains and enjoy the treasures that humor brings.

Happy Prospecting!

Unconventional Wisdom

Why aren't the comics and inspirational stories spread throughout the paper instead of being buried at the end? If the spreading technique were used, then instead of contributing to heavy hearts, newspapers could actually lighten them.

Be a Grin Reaper

One of my friend's greatest joys in life is to be what he calls a *grin reaper*. Actually, I think he laughs harder at his jokes than anyone else does, but that's okay…two smiles are better than one. His intent is also one of the most noble: to enhance the quality of another person's day. You too can be a grin reaper.

Reflection Quote

I'm the kind of person who's so optimistic that if I was on the Titanic, I would have thought we were stopping for ice.

—Unknown

Share-Ware

There is a common term in the vernacular of the computer world: *share-ware*. This is software that anyone can use for free. Quite a deal. Well, I have news for those in the computer crowd: theirs is not the first share-ware.

Humor was the original share-ware. Think about it. What do you do immediately after you hear a new joke or funny story? You go out and share it with someone else.

Reflection Quote

God put me on this earth to accomplish a certain number of things. Right now I'm so far behind, I will never die.

—Unknown

Not that the joke always stays funny. There's always the person who says "Oh, I heard a great joke the other day" but can't remember how it goes. But what's important is that even people with "joke-forgetting genes" *want* to share the joke. Sorry, back to share-ware. Humor is wonderful because it is meant to be shared. You can tailor jokes and stories to match the intended audience, and then in turn the listeners will tailor it for their audiences, and so on. The joke or story today is very different than when it was originally conceived. This is called *humor evolution*. The great thing about humor evolution is that a lot of folks have their humor bones touched along the way.

Appropriate Humor

The appropriateness of humor is always an issue for discussion. There is a good rule of thumb for this. (Why is it a thumb and not an index finger?) The rule of thumb is: if the humor hurts or degrades another individual or a collective group of people, then it is inappropriate. This is one instance where you need to be even more sensitive to others than usual. The positive side of humor, however, is that there is an abundance of it in this world, so there's plenty for you to share without diminishing others in some manner for a laugh.

Different Jokes for Different Folks

This section is especially for all of you who have inherited the joke-forgetting genes. You thought you were off of the hook, didn't you? Please hear this announcement. Just because you can't tell a standard joke doesn't mean that you can't be a humorous person. You can still tell *your* stories, you can deliver one-liners in response to some comment or event, you can describe humorous happenings you witnessed or heard about. These are all humor avenues you can travel. Don't give up on humor just because you can't tell a joke.

A corollary to this is to *not* listen to yourself when you say "I'm not a funny person." Grab that selective-perception Geiger counter and those prospecting glasses and you will find that you *are* a funny person…but in your own unique way. "Unique" funny is a whole lot better than canned, scripted funny. Discover your unique humor abilities and you can add smiles to your life.

Complete-a-PHI

No, PHI is not a Greek sorority or honor society. Rather, it is a Personal Humor Inventory. Take a moment and complete this one.

Personal Humor Inventory

1. What are three things that make me laugh?

   a. _____

   b. _____

   c. _____

2. What humorous media (comics, movies, music, books) do I intentionally seek?

   a. _____

   b. _____

   c. _____

3. What methods of humor am I most comfortable with? Circle one.

   a. Jokes

   b. Funny stories

   c. One-liners

   d. Other (that's wide open, isn't it!)

4. When I discover something funny, this is how hard I laugh. (Circle one.)

   a. Giggle

   b. Chortle

   c. Cry

   d. Belly jiggle

   e. Earthquake shock wave

   f. Internal quiet murmur

   g. Depends

5. What is one thing that I can do to increase my humor quotient? (This one you can write out.)

   _____

   _____

   _____

   _____

PHI note: Understanding your relationship to humor is critical in the humor growth process. Challenge yourself to be a smile creator.

Laugh at Yourself, Before...

A friend of mine told me the following true story about himself. He had just been appointed Acting President of our university. One morning he was gearing up for a big day. He was sitting at the breakfast table with his 10-year-old son. His son asked what he was doing today. My friend replied, "Well, today is one of the biggest days in my career. I've got to give a speech to about 650 people and get them excited about our future together." The son looked at his dad, and with a straight face said, "Well, you better zip up your zipper then." Sure enough, my friend's zipper was down.

Unconventional Wisdom

Once you get people laughing, they're listening and you can tell them most anything.

—Herb Gardner

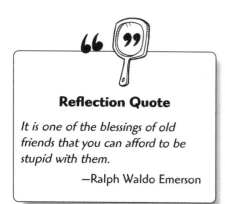

Reflection Quote

It is one of the blessings of old friends that you can afford to be stupid with them.

—Ralph Waldo Emerson

My friend went to work. He addressed the crowd of 650 employees and immediately recounted the breakfast-table story, after which the crowd roared with laughter.

Laugh at yourself.

There are several internal benefits of laughing at yourself. Here are two...you can probably think of some of your own.

➤ **Perfectionism Antidote.** Perfectionism can be a demon, raising its ugly head and leaving doubt about self-worth. Well, the ADAA (American Demons-Abolisher Association) has great news for you! Laughing at yourself, in a non-demoning way, is the ideal antidote for perfectionism. By laughing at yourself, you give yourself permission to make mistakes. By laughing at yourself, you take off the chains of seriousness. Sure, seriousness is OK and at times essential, but when it dominates your life you lose the thrill.

➤ **Perspective Keeper.** Laughing at yourself also helps you keep life's obstacles in perspective. The nature of being human means that you will have some struggles; laughter helps soften the bumps. Laughter is a great perspective enhancer.

There are also external benefits of laughing at yourself.

➤ **Create a Bond with Others.** Public speakers have known for years that if you use self-deprecating humor, you can strengthen the bond with your audience. That is exactly what my friend did with his zipper story. When you laugh at yourself, you present yourself as a real person, not a stuffed-shirt, unfeeling robot. Folks in the audience can relate to you person-to-person. After all, they probably have made one or two mistakes themselves.

➤ **Role model.** Another benefit of laughing at yourself in public (I'm not talking about doing it alone on a street in New York City) is that you're serving as a role model for others. It gives them permission to laugh at themselves...a great gift to give others, when you think about it.

Laughter: A Healthy Choice

Americans spend millions of dollars every year on health clubs, health foods, health plans, while one of the greatest preventers of disease and illness...*laughter*...is right under their noses. And it is free!

Study after study (in the layperson's vernacular, that means a lot of studies) has effectively demonstrated the positive power of laughter in our lives, both emotionally and physically. I won't repeat the studies here because I know that you will want to test the idea for yourself some day. I'm prepared to write you a prescription for healthier living. But first I must confess: I'm not a *real* doctor. At least that is what my daughter told me when she was eight. She said, "Dad, you're not a real doctor because you can't write notes so people can go get medicine." Try explaining academic doctoral credentials to an eight-year-old. I quickly found out that I just ought to admit that I'm not a real doctor.

So, since I can't prescribe pharmaceutical drugs, I prescribe another type of drug, one of the most potent around...laughter.

I am not one of those doctors who prescribes synthetic laughter. The type I prescribe is all natural, which is much healthier, and dosage size doesn't matter. I've never heard of anyone overdosing on laughter.

Beware of canned laughter. Canned laughter has the key nutrients processed out...like the part that includes the genuine funny bone. You want to make wholesome and hearty humor a staple in your diet.

The actual prescription follows:

YES!

Power Plate

BHUMORS

Reflection Quote

Happiness is good health and a bad memory.

—Ingrid Bergman

YES!

Power Plate

LAFALOT

Good Humor Prescription

Directions: At least 3 times a day take a generous dose of wholesome laughter. It can be derived from life, jokes, movies, comics, music, or literature. When the laughter hits you, repress all urges to stifle it, as doing so will minimize the positive impact of this powerful medicine. Let the laughter escape...loud and clear. Laughter is more important than etiquette, so make it *big*.

Repeat daily for the rest of your life, which with laughter will be long and fruitful.

Indications: For the recurrent feeling of euphoria, due to the sensations associated with laughter. Smile may expand, body may tense, and gentle body-shaking may occur. Side benefit: stress will be reduced.

Caution: Belly laughs can cause snorting and flailing of the arms and hands. Make sure there is ample room to protect others from your humor movements. At some points in your life, a higher dosage may be required to help you cope with life's difficulties.

Interactions: Extreme laughter with others could result in strong life-long relationships.

Tamper Persistent: Feel free to tamper with humor and instill it in others.

200 calories expended per each laugh.

Rx: CRE8LAFTRNYORLIF4THHLTHOVIT

The Least You Need to Know

➤ You already have the tools to prospect for humor.

➤ Share your humor: two smiles are better than one.

➤ Humor-us and thyself.

➤ The humor diet is hearty, wholesome, and healthy.

Chapter 15

Perform the Great Balancing Act

In This Chapter

➤ How to benefit your body

➤ How to enrich your mind

➤ How to nourish your soul

➤ How to contribute to your community

Fast faxes. Late-night meetings. Chauffeuring kids. Bumper-to-bumper traffic. Cellular phones. Tight budgets. Dual-career couples. Project deadlines. All are signs of the times. So how do you cope with the many demands pulling at you from so many directions? How do you achieve optimal living? How do you feel fulfilled? How do you enhance your own self-esteem?

Tough questions, yes. But you have what it takes to address them. This type of introspection and change takes work, realistic self-assessment, and a commitment to growth. I said it wouldn't be easy.

First of all, you must recognize that the key to life success is balance of "the big four": body, spirit, mind, and community. The big four are the threads that make up your life tapestry. If you leave out some of the threads, or don't pay attention to which ones are used where and when, then the tapestry is weakened and optimal living cannot be achieved. To create optimal living, you need to become a master weaver. Grab your yarn and weave on!

Inspirational Injection

Wellness: Getting Started

I spent a fortune

On a trampoline,

A stationary bike

And a rowing machine,

Complete with gadgets

To read my pulse,

And gadgets to prove

My progress results,

And others to show

The miles I've charted—

But they left off the gadget

To get me started!

—Unknown

Body Fit: One Size Does Not Fit All

Imagine this scenario. You are sitting on your favorite chair, watching TV with your feet appropriately propped up. It's January 1, and you're feeling that extra 15 pounds you've invested your money in over the holidays. Now, for some reason the beer commercials alternate with the "get fit" commercials. (I think that the commercial industry is conspiring to keep Americans in the fat-thin cycle.)

OK. It's time for the New Year's resolution. It's time to get back into shape (*what* shape I'm not sure). So you begin your rigorous exercise program, and you go at it hard.

Fast-forward your life to January 15th. Two weeks have gone by, you are sitting on your favorite chair, with your feet appropriately propped up. One of those "get fit" commercials comes on the TV. You say to yourself, "Well, I tried. It just didn't work out."

You are now eligible to be a member of the "Tried to Get Fit Club." This club enjoys a membership of millions—in fact, it boasts larger numbers than any organization in the world. Your membership entitles you to all the rights and privileges afforded those who say, "I tried"—heart attacks, obesity, strokes, shortness of breath, fragile bones, and much more.

It's a harsh reality, but you know it's true.

Volkswagen Attitude

Kenneth Pelletier, a healthy author (or is that an author about health?), says that we have a "Volkswagen Attitude." What we do is drive ourselves and drive ourselves until we break. Then we expect that we can go to the doctor and get fixed.

"So what are the problems with this attitude?" you might ask. Thank you for asking. Here are just a few:

1. The parts are harder to get.
2. The parts are more fragile and much more difficult to install.
3. Too often, you don't get a second chance. You can't fix it. The heart attack or stroke kills or permanently disables you.

It's time for a little attitude adjustment.

Commit Yourself to a Preventatorium

Preventatorium admission price: commitment. A Preventatorium is a place you can go to prevent disease or illness from happening to you. Now, unlike the Preventatoriums of old with their walled structures, the type I'm talking about is a frame of mind. Prevention begins and ends with you.

Sometimes prevention is an attitude that is hard to grasp, because there is no reward at a specific point in time associated with prevention. Human beings want rewards. Your reward is long-term, not immediate, and this sometimes makes prevention more difficult.

Power Plate

Postvention Syndrome

Too often, people get the prevention attitude *after* a negative health event—this is called *postvention*. Unfortunately, often the damage has already been done.

Here's the challenge you can give yourself. If you are prone to the postvention syndrome, then before there is an actual physical illness, visualize what life would be like with a physical illness. Use that mental image as your catalyst to disown the postvention attitude and embrace—fully—the prevention state of mind!

Become Your Own Aerobic Ally

Kenneth H. Cooper, the cardio guru and researcher, brought the word *aerobics* into our living rooms and exercise regimes. You hear the word all the time and know that it is good for the heart—but what does it really do?

Here is some information so that you can present yourself as an exercise expert at the next cocktail party you attend. This is the cocktail synthesis of the research (the information comes from actual research, but the scientific nomenclature has been omitted to prevent the cocktail "eyes-glazed-over" expression).

Here's how it works. You walk up to someone at the party and the conversation begins. During the conversation, you slightly bend your knee and wince, making sure the person you are talking with sees the action. That person, being empathic and sensitive, says "Are you OK?" You say, "Yes, my knee is just a little sore from running." "Oh, you are a runner." You continue, "Yes, I do it for the aerobic benefit." Now here is where you begin the exercise-expert lesson.

"You know, there are some incredible benefits to being aerobically fit:

1. You increase the number of capillaries in your body.

2. You increase the flexibility of your lungs.

3. You strengthen your heart muscle.

4. You increase the healing capacity of your body.

5. And for the pièce de résistance, you increase the amount of blood in your body by an entire quart—from five quarts to six quarts."

The person you are talking with says, "That is incredible."

You respond, "Yes, and all that for only one hour a week. By exercising three times a week for 20 minutes, you can add quality to your life. You should see a physician first and create a fitness program with a personal trainer, to be on the safe side."

The cardio cocktail conversation *always* works, unless of course you strike up a conversation with someone who happens to be a cardiologist. At that point, unless you want to discuss the latest research from the *New England Journal of Medicine*, you probably want to excuse yourself and go talk with someone who is not a doctor.

Power Plate

AROBX4U

Unconventional Wisdom

Exercise you enjoy—is exercise you employ.

Visit the Pyramid

For centuries, people have visited the pyramids to seek wisdom and understanding. Wouldn't it be great to visit one? Well, now you can, and the fare is free: zero, zip, nada. Your virtual trip can take you to the Food Pyramid.

It has incredible treasures, there are no hieroglyphics to decipher, and it can provide you insights and wisdom. There are myriad benefits to be reaped from the pyramid, which was created by our own federal government. Good job, governmentors!

Daily Food Guide Pyramid.

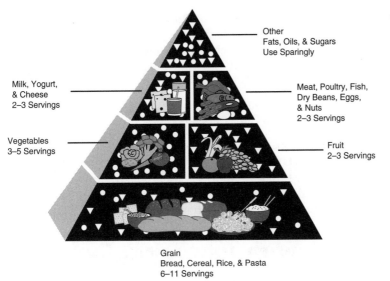

Other
Fats, Oils, & Sugars
Use Sparingly

Milk, Yogurt,
& Cheese
2–3 Servings

Meat, Poultry, Fish,
Dry Beans, Eggs,
& Nuts
2–3 Servings

Vegetables
3–5 Servings

Fruit
2–3 Servings

Grain
Bread, Cereal, Rice, & Pasta
6–11 Servings

One of the major benefits of this pyramid is the set of guidelines superimposed on the pyramid's structure. These guidelines can assist you as you prepare for your weekly eating adventures.

Think about how helpful these guidelines can be. Do you ever ask yourself or your spouse, "What should we have for dinner tonight?" Well, travel to your pyramid and you already have some preset clues. Right in front of your very eyes, the pyramid instructs you about what is needed and the number of servings required.

Unconventional Wisdom

Eat foods as close to the original source as possible.

—Kenneth Pelletier

Nutrition Nudge

Why do you need a nutrition nudge? Let's look at it this way. Do you ever not pay attention to the food that fuels your body? Do you ever get into a fast-food rut? Do you ever get the ice cream addiction?

The point of the nutrition nudge is to increase your awareness of what and how much of what you are putting into your body. Once you are aware, then you can make the necessary positive changes.

Now, I'm not advocating that you become "all natural." However, if you incorporate a philosophy of moderation and believe you can significantly improve your nutritional self, your body will say thanks!

Body Image

Americans have been obsessed with body image throughout the ages, often to the detriment of their own well-being. For years we had Barbie, the perfect-bodied role model. No one (at least no one I know) could ever match up to the doll. Realistic body image is a tough concept, but when you truly accept your body image, you can have a much happier life.

Back to Barbie. Even she has changed. Instead of her exaggeratedly thin and busty body of yesteryear, she now looks much more like real people.

Don't emulate a doll, don't emulate a person—you need to discover the body image that is in concert with your individual uniqueness. Some of your attributes you can change (hair, weight, vocabulary), but don't change in an attempt to be accepted by others. Accept yourself and recognize your own attractiveness.

Reflection Quote

At feasts, remember that you are entertaining two guests, body and soul. What you give to your body you soon lose; what you give to the soul, you keep forever.

—Epictetus

Nourish Your Spirit: Curb the Hunger

People are starving for a sense of soul. You see this as you peruse bookstore shelves—books relating to soul are in abundance as never before. This search for soul is not a fad, but rather a statement of spiritual emptiness. When is the last time you took steps to discover some aspect of your soul?

Soul Architecture

The architecture of people is interesting: composed of mind, body, community, and soul. Think about how much time you spend working on the physical structure—exercising, dieting, coloring your hair (if you have hair), and decorating your frame with fabrics. You also spend a lot of time cultivating your intellect, which is obvious because you are reading *this* book.

For many people, however, the soul remains a mystery waiting to be unleashed so that it can serve as a force to guide their lives. Why are we reluctant to search for self, to uncover the riches of our souls? Is it because our lives have been so cluttered with information, quick facts, fast decisions, and dizzying paces that we think we don't have time for soul discovery, and it merely gets in the way? What do you think?

Do you stay away from soul development because it is such a difficult task? Maybe because the answers are not concrete? Maybe because you are afraid of the unknown? Uncertainty will be a partner in the soul-development process.

When we go to work, we invest ourselves in analyzing data, but we often forget to invest in analysis of ourselves: personal introspection. This kind of soul development is difficult, but it provides the perspective needed to make the most effective and balanced life decisions.

Power Plate

ESPIRIT

Extra, Extra—Hear All About It

Lend me your ears. This soul business is critical business. Don't let your sense of urgency, your business pressures, your ladder-climbing distractions, and concern for things over people let you lose touch with your souls. When you do, the results are apathy, dissension, unhappiness, chaos, and disenchanted living.

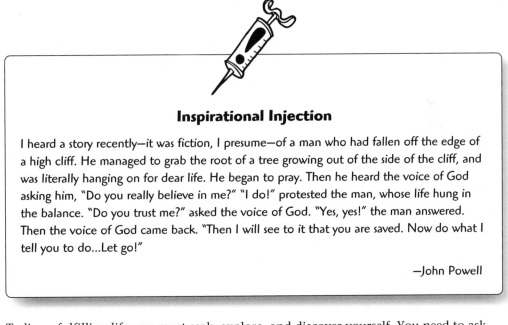

Inspirational Injection

I heard a story recently—it was fiction, I presume—of a man who had fallen off the edge of a high cliff. He managed to grab the root of a tree growing out of the side of the cliff, and was literally hanging on for dear life. He began to pray. Then he heard the voice of God asking him, "Do you really believe in me?" "I do!" protested the man, whose life hung in the balance. "Do you trust me?" asked the voice of God. "Yes, yes!" the man answered. Then the voice of God came back. "Then I will see to it that you are saved. Now do what I tell you to do...Let go!"

—John Powell

To live a fulfilling life you must seek, explore, and discover yourself. You need to ask yourself difficult questions such as:

➤ Who am I?

➤ What is my purpose in life?

➤ What are my values?

➤ How can I make a difference in my family, my work, and my community?

Boy, these questions are tough! Struggle with the answers, search for the meaning, give yourself permission not to have to come up with an immediate, concrete response. What you will find is that the more you grapple with questions like these, the more your sense of self will crystallize and solidify. The caveat is that the answers will constantly change—as you do.

Cultivate Your Marvelous Mind

Imagine this scenario. It's graduation day. The graduation speaker (she has to be over 100 years old), gets up to the lectern, and in a quavery, gravelly voice says, "Today is not the end of your education, but rather the beginning." Have you ever heard that line before? Of course you have: it is the requisite line used in every graduation speech from the time of Sophocles to today. The response to that line is also a required response—the graduates roll their eyes. They are thinking, "Hey, I just finished four or five or six years of school and this person is telling me that I've just begun. Help!"

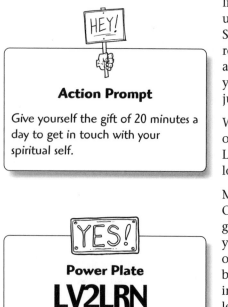

Action Prompt

Give yourself the gift of 20 minutes a day to get in touch with your spiritual self.

Power Plate

LV2LRN

Well, I'm going to have to take the side of the 100+year-old graduation speaker. You really *have* just begun. Learning is a life-long proposition—so I hope your life is long.

Many years ago I heard a story about Cato—no not O.J.'s friend, but Cato the Roman philosopher. I have to go on hearsay because I wasn't born until a couple of years after Cato. Apparently, when Cato was 80 years old, he decided he was going to learn Greek. When his buddies found out, they went to him and said, probably in unison, "Cato, why in the world would you want to learn Greek at such a late age?" Stroking his philosopher-like beard, he wisely replied, "80 is the earliest age I've got."

Courageous Commitment

Right now is the earliest age *you've* got—to make a commitment to life-long learning, to grow yourself. And when you grow yourself, who are the beneficiaries? You and everyone whose life you touch—and you touch many lives every single day.

The list of things you can do to be the ultimate cultivator is endless. However, to help you get started, I'll provide some:

➤ Take a class.

➤ Visit the library.

➤ Go to a museum.

➤ Visit a foreign country.

➤ Take half-day adventure road trips.

➤ Read magazines on topics out of your area of expertise.

These are the best mind stimulants!

Reflection Quote

A person's mind stretched by a new idea never goes back to its original dimensions.

—Oliver Wendell Holmes

Second that Emotion

What a great lyric for a song. Oh yeah, somebody already used it....Oh well.

Emotions are an essential facet of the mind, in terms of this life-balance concept. But, since all of Part 3 is already devoted to emotions, I'll save you the repetition and merely—second the emotion.

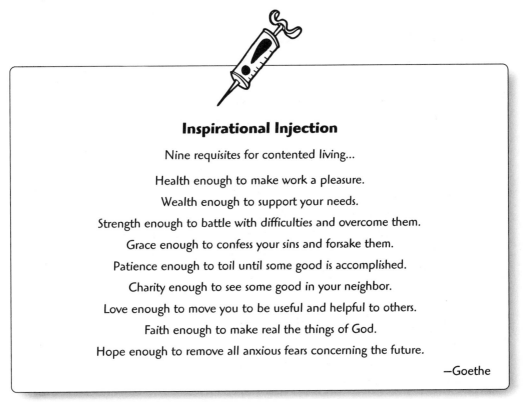

Inspirational Injection

Nine requisites for contented living...

Health enough to make work a pleasure.

Wealth enough to support your needs.

Strength enough to battle with difficulties and overcome them.

Grace enough to confess your sins and forsake them.

Patience enough to toil until some good is accomplished.

Charity enough to see some good in your neighbor.

Love enough to move you to be useful and helpful to others.

Faith enough to make real the things of God.

Hope enough to remove all anxious fears concerning the future.

—Goethe

True Community Is a Feeling—Not a Location

Zip code, city name, street address—attributes the Postal Service uses to determine *"community."* In fact, a quick perusal of a variety of dictionaries will indicate that the first definition of community is precisely this—related to location. (Don't let someone see you perusing dictionaries; they might think that you don't have a life.)

The second definition of community has to do with sharing something in common—the *feeling* aspect of community. With all due respect to the dictionary writers, because I wouldn't want the task of writing definitions, I feel that these definitions are backwards in terms of importance.

Unconventional Wisdom

How many persons we meet in houses, whom we scarcely speak to, whom yet we know, and who know us. How many we see in the street, or sit with in church, whom though silently, we warmly rejoice to be with.

—Ralph Waldo Emerson

First and foremost, true community is a feeling, not a location. I'm sure there've been many times when you lived in a particular location, or belonged to a church or other group, when you did not feel part of the community even though you were called a member. Location and affiliation do not ensure a sense of community.

Let's go a step farther. The dictionary writers omitted a very significant aspect of community. Community, defined as location, is simple. You are either physically in the community or not. Easy. Community defined as a feeling or sense of belonging, however, is incredibly difficult to accomplish. It takes time and commitment to truly become part of a community.

Why Is Community so Important?

Community is important for so many reasons.

➤ It meets our interdependency needs.

➤ It capitalizes on the synergy created.

➤ It strengthens the bonds of relationships.

➤ It enhances respect for one another.

➤ It enriches our collective quality of life.

Get Back to Life

Years ago I was watching a Peter, Paul, and Mary concert on TV. During one of the song breaks, they decided to insert some social commentary that really had an impact on the way I view community. They used magazine titles to reflect how our society and relationships with one another have changed over the years:

1. In the 1950s we had the magazine *Life*.
2. In the 1960s we had the magazine *People*.
3. In the 1970s we had the magazine *Us*.
4. In the 1980s we had the magazine *Self*.

Peter, Paul, and Mary were right. We have changed, and what we need to do as a society is to get back to *Life*, looking at ourselves in the context of the larger community. Individuals and communities are interdependent and cannot survive without each other.

Reflection Quote

I have noticed that when chickens quit quarreling over their food, they often find that there is enough for all of them. I wonder if it might not be the same for the human race.

—Don Marquis

Make the Community Commitment

True community is not something external—it is not "them." Community is me, you, us. By becoming involved and sharing your talents, you can become a community treasure.

Take a moment and think about your particular community. What arouses your passion? Education? Service organizations? Kids? The environment? Translate your internal passion into community action. Do not undervalue your gifts, because by giving of yourself you are making the greatest contribution.

Reflection Quote

The influence of a beautiful, helpful, hopeful, character is contagious and may revolutionize a whole town.

—Eleanor Porter

Benefits of Community Involvement

The more you get involved with your community, the more you and those around you will profit.

➤ You will meet some incredible people.
➤ You will learn many things.
➤ You will make a difference.
➤ You will enrich the lives of others.
➤ You will assume greater ownership of your community.
➤ You will have *fun!*

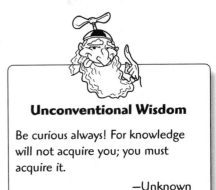

Unconventional Wisdom

Be curious always! For knowledge will not acquire you; you must acquire it.

—Unknown

The Least You Need to Know

➤ Fit your body for optimal living.

➤ Treasure your mind.

➤ Your soul gives you purpose.

➤ You and your community are interdependent.

Part 6
Exercise Decision-Making: Exercise Without the Sweat

I have always been delighted at the prospect of a new day, a fresh try, one more start, with perhaps a bit of magic waiting somewhere behind the morning.

J. B. Priestly

How have you lost the power to choose? Do you make everything in your life the responsibility of others? Do you cripple yourself with shoulds? You can take a new approach to decision-making. As you do so, you'll find that many things you take for granted can be called into question and challenged: you'll build new and deeper connections with others, questioning previous parameters and choosing new ones.

Chapter 16

Take the Choice Challenge

In This Chapter

➤ How to become a dynamic decision-maker

➤ Discover your control locus focus

➤ How to make ethical decisions

➤ Whose choice is it anyway?

Decisions, decisions, decisions. From what to eat to what to wear. From where to socialize to where to go to school. From what to believe to what to be. How many decisions do you think you make in a day? Last I counted (and boy was I tired when I finished) it was in the hundreds of thousands. Now that is *some* decision-making!

An interesting facet of decision-making is that the vast majority of our decisions are made at a subconscious level. Many are the result of habit (when to brush teeth, for example), while others result from a physiological keep-safe response. Yet others are from learning gained from previous experiences. All these decisions keep us functioning, minute to minute.

The conscious decisions are like the tip of an iceberg. These are the decisions in our conscious field of vision and experience, the ones we focus on and consider when we think about decision-making. They number considerably less than our subconscious decisions, but they consume a lot more of our energy.

Are you ready to read on? You decide.

Choices: Own 'Em

We all want ownership. We want to own our own home. We want to own our own car. We live in the land of acquisition. We want to own...except sometimes when it comes to our choices. If you own your choices, then you have to accept *responsibility*, and sometimes that's scary.

Actually, your choice is the greatest thing you can own. You are the artist and your choices are the hues you put on your life canvas. Create it...*now!*

Power Plate

UCHUSE

Unconventional Wisdom

One of the interesting paradoxes in life is "I want choice but I don't want to choose."

Reflection Quote

Happiness is a conscious choice, not an automatic response.

—Mildred Barthel

Scapegoats Anonymous

Remember when your Mom or Dad used to make decisions for you? You complained, but many times, deep down, you were glad they made the decisions. Then you didn't have to own them, you didn't have to be responsible—and most important, it was *their fault* when a decision didn't work out and *your* victory when it did.

Aah, yes, the great scapegoat. If other people make a decision for you, you are not accountable for it—they are. Then you get to say, "It didn't work out because *they* made the decision." The proverbial "they" become the scapegoat.

If you are unhappy, unfulfilled, dissatisfied with life, and you have scapegoats, then you can blame your terrible life on someone else. What a shame.

The fact is that while you want to point the finger elsewhere, most of your fingers are actually pointing right back at you. You are totally responsible for your well-being. Reframe your decision-thinking. Look at decisions as opportunities to create a life adventure. You not only have control, you have total control. Let the scapegoat escape!

Land of the Shoulds

When I was in college, a professor told me that many people live in the Land of the Shoulds. The people there are a miserable lot. They do everything because they *ought* to do it or they *should* do it.

These inhabitants make decisions because of obligations and coercion. The taxes you pay in this land are a diminished sense of self and a surrendering of your own personhood.

When you live in the Land of the Shoulds, your decisions are made for an external public, not for yourself. You live other people's aspirations and dreams. The challenge is to live your own dreams. As my wise professor always said, "You need to quit shoulding on yourself."

Locus of Control: Internal, External, Nocturnal

Consider this scenario. You walk into the hardware store of life. After you get your cart to carry all your new tools, you start to look at the overhead signs to find the decision aisle. Upon finding the decision aisle you look for the Locus of Control section. You ease up to the section and discover three types: internal, external, and nocturnal. Since you are an astute life shopper, you compare the contents of the three types. Attention shoppers: locus of control contents always read in the first person.

➤ **Internal Locus of Control:** I have the power. I take control. My decisions are made from within. I make decisions from my soul. My decisions are the intersection of my beliefs, behaviors, and words. I determine my future and my life. I don't react, I act. I am a proactor.

➤ **Nocturnal Locus of Control:** I sleepwalk through life. I toss and turn. I don't deal with reality. I live through night dreams as if I'm an actor in a movie. I wander aimlessly. Life is great until I wake up, except for an occasional nightmare. I am a sleeper.

➤ **External Locus of Control:** You have the power over me. External influences control my life. I make decisions based on what others want. My life and future are determined by outside sources. I am a reactor.

Unconventional Wisdom

Keep away from people who try to belittle your ambitions. Small people always do that, but the really great make you feel that you, too, can be great.

—Mark Twain

Reflection Quote

The good we do today becomes the happiness of tomorrow.

—Chinese proverb

So you've reviewed the contents. Which locus of control do you choose? A good way to examine locus of control is to view it as a continuum with internal on one end and external on the other end. "Nocturnal" just floats around the cosmos somewhere.

Are there times when your internal locus of control takes charge more, and other times when the external takes over? When are these times?

List three feelings or circumstances in which your internal locus of control is in charge.

1. _____

2. _____

3. _____

List three feelings or circumstances when your external locus of control is in charge.

1. _____

2. _____

3. _____

Now here is the ultimate test. On the locus of control continuum, mark where you spend most of your time.

Internal <————————————————————————————> External

The goal is to move more toward the internal side of the continuum. Take charge of your life!

Inspirational Injection

Up against a wall?

You can stare at it.

You can destroy it.

You can scale it.

Or you can create a window.

—Unknown

Accept, Don't Except

Accept the ability to choose. You are the pilot of your life. You're the one flipping the switches, feeding the data, pressing the buttons, stewarding the emotions, and maintaining equilibrium. If you don't take the role as pilot you will become lost. You might end up where someone else wants you to be, but not necessarily where you want to be.

When you "except" choices or exclude yourself from responsibility for your direction, you pay. The cost is unfulfilled living.

Control Paradox

Although you need to take control, to accept responsibility for your choices, there are many events in life you cannot control, such as weather, death, financial markets, and hemlines. At this point your choice becomes "How do I react to this event?" Your reaction is what you have control over in this scenario. Control it.

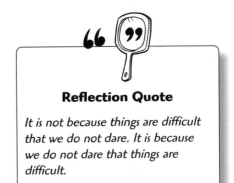

Reflection Quote

It is not because things are difficult that we do not dare. It is because we do not dare that things are difficult.

—Seneca

Unscramble Ramble

Take the word LOCUS and unscramble it to discover the hidden direction it gives you to help in the decision-making process. (Take two minutes to unscramble.)

_____

_____

You came up with some great attempts. Here is one that I hope will help:

C SOUL

When you're making decisions you should always consult your soul. This reinforces your use of internal locus of control, while at the same time enhancing the integrity of your decisions.

Power Plate

MNKNTRL

The Low-Down on Decisions

It's decision time. Hmm. Let's see. What types are there? Consensus, democratic, autocratic, feeling, thinking, default, short-term, long-term. I'm not going to go over all the different types. That would be overwhelming—at least for me. My goal is to simplify the emotionally laden event called "decision-making."

Let's talk process. Here is a process model that will help you make any type of decision. This model synthesizes the work of philosophers and dynamic decision makers from yesteryear to today.

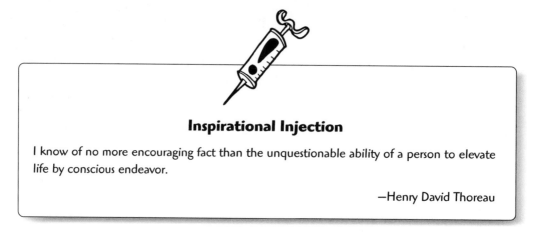

Inspirational Injection

I know of no more encouraging fact than the unquestionable ability of a person to elevate life by conscious endeavor.

—Henry David Thoreau

Dynamic Decision-Making Model

Here is the five-part dynamic decision-making model.

1. Determine whether a decision is an ethical one or the highly sophisticated "regular" decision. If it is an ethical decision, proceed to step 2. If it is a regular decision skip to step 5.

2. If it is a decision involving ethics, work through the three moral inventory questions (described in the bulleted list below).

3. If you have decided that the decision is ethical and should be carried out, then proceed to step 5 and use the "regular" decision steps (described below). If you conclude that following through with the decision is not ethical, proceed to step 4.

4. Stop. Don't do it.

5. Follow the steps required of the "regular" decision-making process.

It's never easy to decide whether a particular course of action is "ethical." After all, everyone has a different set of guidelines to follow. Whose criteria do you use? Below is my own approach to help simplify the process and distill complex decision-making to a few basic rules. These three questions can be a practical guide to everyday ethical decision-making. The questions posed in this moral inventory are:

➤ **Does it nurture my identity?** Think about the Integrity Trinity mentioned elsewhere in this book. Does the action that I am considering fit my deepest convictions, the identity I want other people to believe about me, and other actions of mine that I value?

➤ **Is it a genuine solution?** Would an objective observer say that the action would achieve what it is supposed to achieve? Or is it just a self-serving action, or one that helps me sidestep the real issue?

➤ **Does it nurture my community?** Does it fit my community's ideals? And will doing it strengthen my ties to the community or create division? Remember that "community" can be defined in a number of ways. Not every moral action will make all our neighbors happy. But each action should nurture whatever we understand as our community: our religious institution, educational institution, business, support group, and so forth.

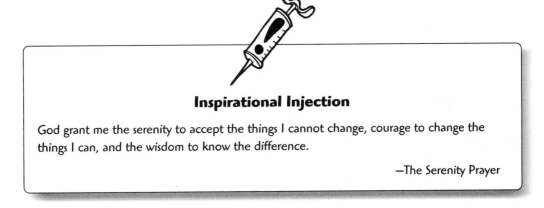

Inspirational Injection

God grant me the serenity to accept the things I cannot change, courage to change the things I can, and the wisdom to know the difference.

—The Serenity Prayer

Let's move on to the regular decision-making process based on the work of decision-making theorists and pragmatists (you ought to see those two groups get together for a discussion). This eight-step offering will help you with your own decision-making:

1. Define the problem.

2. Gather information. Obtain information from as many sources as you can. The more you rely on your own information, the less effective your decision will be.

3. Develop alternative solutions. Challenge yourself to design several. Don't just go with the first one that seems plausible. By having a variety from which to choose, you can make the better choice.

4. Examine the consequences of each solution.

5. Take the 24-hour escape break (see the next section on intuition).

Action Prompt

Memorize my three moral inventory questions (above) now. This will only take a few minutes, but will serve you for a lifetime.

165

6. Revisit the problem and make sure you have defined it properly.

7. Implement the decision and follow through.

8. Assess and learn from the decision you made.

Intuition Infusion

Refer to step 5 in the previous section. It says, "Take the 24-hour escape break." This step is especially critical for the big decisions that hang over your head like a storm cloud in April. Absorb as much decision information as you can, and focus all your energies on solving the problem. Then, if the decision still eludes you, it's time for the 24-hour escape break.

Power Plate

DCIDEIT

Give yourself permission to put the problem out of your mind—completely out of your consciousness. Every time it attempts to creep back, shove it out. This will foster the subconscious synergistic effect of your intuition and logic, allowing them to work their magic.

When you take the break, you free neural pathways and promote a different level of processing. This practice will often lead to the Aha! Moment—the lightbulb effect of a decision being birthed.

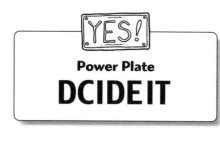

Unconventional Wisdom

Life offers two gifts—time and ability to choose how we spend it. Planning is a process of choosing among those many options. If we do not choose to plan, then we choose to have others plan for us.

—Richard Winwood

Second-Guessing Gastritis

Have you ever made a decision and then gone through the ol' second-guessing routine?

➤ I should have made the other decision.

➤ I don't know why I didn't make the other choice.

➤ This decision will not get me where I want to be.

➤ I know this decision won't work out.

Then you drop it, only to pick it up the next day. And the questions start again. "Should I have..."

When you begin to feel the tearing sensation in the lining of your stomach or the acid assault of your gastric juices, then you know you've got it: Second-Guessing Gastritis.

Why is it that you won't let go of decisions you've made? Why do you need to continually resurrect the turmoil of assuming that the decision you've made is wrong?

Could it be that you are afraid to succeed? Maybe it is that you want to avoid the responsibility of actually making the decision work out.

Whatever the reason, the time is now that you need to dip into the life medicine cabinet and take a generous dose of the "Second-Guessing Anti-Gastritis Elixir." This elixir will help soothe your stomach, ease your mind, and enhance your decision confidence.

The 16-ounce elixir is made of the following:

2 oz. let-go of past alternatives.

1 oz. focus on the decision you did make.

3 oz. put steps in action to carry out your decision.

2 oz. focus on positive outcomes of the decision.

3 oz. get support from others in helping you make the decision come to fruition.

5 oz. trust your gut (or your intuition, as the sophisticates would say).

The fact is that every decision could be second-guessed. You can spend your whole life in the realm of "what if I made the other decision?" This does nothing but waste energy and drain you of precious resources that you need to move to successful outcomes.

The more you second-guess, the more likely it is you will not fulfill your dreams. Second-guessing is actually self-realization sabotage. There are enough obstacles that life presents. We don't need to be party to internal sabotage efforts.

Make a calculated decision and *move on!*

Unconventional Wisdom

It's a funny thing about life; if you refuse to accept anything but the very best, you very often get it.

—W. Somerset Maugham

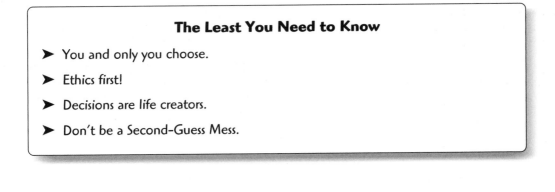

The Least You Need to Know

➤ You and only you choose.

➤ Ethics first!

➤ Decisions are life creators.

➤ Don't be a Second-Guess Mess.

Chapter 17

Become a Resourcerer

In This Chapter

➤ What is your worth?

➤ How do you become an ultimate gem?

➤ How do you nurture networks?

➤ How do you grow your own worth?

Resources—natural, human, intellectual, financial—touch our lives from many angles. They help us enhance our state of living…that is, if we are able to harness their power.

Some resources are worth a whole lot more than others. So how do we measure the worth? Most often we default to the "Simple Economic Paradigm for Evaluating Resource Worth." (Note: if the actual method is as complex as the title, then we are in trouble.)

The figure looks like this:

Economic Paradigm for Evaluating Resource Worth.

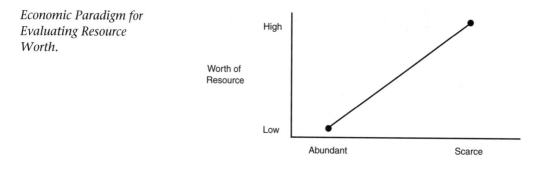

This is a great formula that would make any economist proud. It works very well for inanimate objects and is easy to apply. However, it does not work when we talk about evaluating the worth of an individual. When looking at the human being in terms of resource, we have to start at the high-worth point and go up from there.

You have the potential to transform lives, including your own. You decide how much you increase your personal stock.

Many years ago I served as a counselor for adults. One of my clients, who was suicidal, sought therapy. When asked why she sought therapy, she replied, "I'm here because of my daughter. I'm worthless, but I'm here because I need to provide for her."

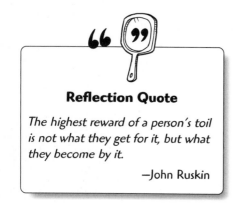

Reflection Quote

The highest reward of a person's toil is not what they get for it, but what they become by it.

—John Ruskin

No one is worthless! Everyone has special gifts, talents, and abilities. The challenge is to tap those attributes, to stimulate their growth and use them for fulfilled living. There are treasures to be discovered, and the time is now.

Let's change the worth evaluation paradigm to fit human beings.

Become a Resourcerer. Seek, find, use, and give your internal resources. Grow your own value by embracing new challenges and grasping new experiences. The more you discover and allow your own uniqueness to come forth, the more incredible your life will become!

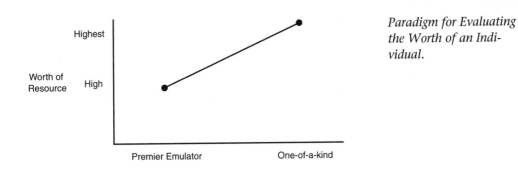

Paradigm for Evaluating the Worth of an Individual.

Be-Rare: The Ultimate Gem Is You

We get excited when we see the facets of a diamond glittering in the light, or the green grandeur permeating the emerald, or the crimson essence emanating from the ruby. We think it would be wonderful to have one of these stellar stones. These are only tangible gems, however, whose purpose is to delight the eye.

There is a much more precious gem in our midst, an intangible gem that delights the spirit and transforms the self. It is the essence of *your* being. Your personhood is a gem that you create by cutting the facets through the power of experience. You are the lapidary. You design the product.

Unlike stone gems that do not change much in value, your value increases as you grow and learn. The more you discover, the more you change, and the more your life worth increases. The experiences you have enhance your rarity. Each new experience adds another facet.

Your lustre brightens with growth. It dulls with stagnated living. It brightens when you adopt an internal locus of control philosophy. It dulls when you let the external locus of control take over.

Polish, cut, create! Today.

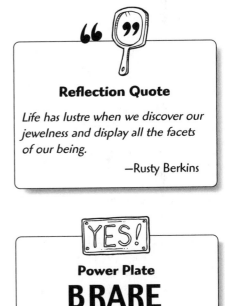

Reflection Quote

Life has lustre when we discover our jewelness and display all the facets of our being.

—Rusty Berkins

YES!

Power Plate

BRARE

Lapidary Lessons

Imagine yourself in the heart of Gem City. You are driving down Lapidary Lane, home of the most inspiring gem shops in the world. The stores' signs wink their neon messages to passers-by. On closer inspection, you discover that the slogans advertising their wares serve as messages you can use to create your most precious gem—*you!*

Here are some Life Lapidaries, slogans for Ultimate Jewelness.

➤ Be a Cut Above the Rest.

➤ Rock Your World.

➤ Bring Lustre to Your Life.

➤ Shaped for Brilliance. Polished for Potential.

➤ Discover Your Fantastic Facets.

➤ Cut, Polish, Reflect...You Are Beautiful.

Power Plate

BNRICHD

Three C's to Gemhood

Neighborhood, knighthood, childhood, sisterhood—did you ever consider gemhood? Yes, gemhood. It is the ability to enhance the preciousness of who you are. To qualify for gemhood you must cultivate the qualities espoused by all gemologists when seeking the ultimate gem: clarity, cut, and color.

Gem Preciousness Checklist

Check those items that apply to you.

Clarity

❑ I have established daily, monthly, and yearly goals.

❑ I undergo periodic values clarification.

❑ I have a clear vision of my future.

❑ I understand my purpose in life.

❑ I keep the cracks and blemishes in perspective.

Cut

❑ I let my reflection touch the lives of others.

❑ I examine my life from different perspectives to understand all of the facets.

❑ I honor the diverse shapes, sizes, and attributes of other gems.

❑ I respect the attributes I have been given.

Color

❑ Different experiences color my reflections of the world.

❑ My hue gives me a unique value.

❑ My environment paints the way I view my world.

❑ The light of learning radiates through me.

Now that you've taken the Gem Checklist, refer back to each quality and form one goal for each.

Reflection Quote

A goal is a dream with a deadline.

—Unknown

1. CLARITY GOAL:

_____

_____

Objective 1:

_____

_____

Objective 2:

_____

_____

This goal will be accomplished by (date): _____

I will celebrate my successful accomplishment the following way:

_____

_____

2. CUT GOAL:

_____

_____

Objective 1:

_____

_____

Objective 2:

_____

_____

This goal will be accomplished by (date): _____

I will celebrate my successful accomplishment the following way:

_____

_____

3. COLOR GOAL:

_____

_____

Objective 1:

_____

_____

Objective 2:

_____

_____

This goal will be accomplished by (date): _____

I will celebrate my successful accomplishment the following way:

_____

_____

Power Plate

TRZUR IT

Unconventional Wisdom

You never know when you are making a memory.

—Rickie Lee Jones

Mine the Treasures Within

Just as any jeweler, gemologist, or lapidary would do, you must take stock of your inventory. Your inventory is a little different than theirs, however, because yours consists of the intangible. Taking inventory of intangible items is no easy task.

Intangible gifts range from art to compassion, from oratory to writing, from listening to creating, from patience to understanding. Unfortunately, you sometimes lose sight of your gifts because of the many demands life places on you. You retreat to a survival mode instead of a revival mode. Let's get to the revival mode. One way to revive your sense of self is to evaluate, appreciate, and articulate your gifts and goals.

First let's evaluate. Get into your search mode. Instead of a WorldWideWeb search, you can get even more sophisticated and do a neural search—the search of the mind, heart, and spirit—which is much more powerful than any computer browser available.

Inspirational Injection

We must delight in each other, make others' conditions our own, rejoice together, mourn together, labor and suffer together, always having before our eyes our community as members of the same body.

—John Winthrop

Inventory

1. If I asked your best friend to share with me three of your greatest gifts, talents, or abilities, what might she or he say?

   ➤ _____

   ➤ _____

   ➤ _____

2. What do *you* think are your three greatest gifts, talents, or abilities?

   ➤ _____

   ➤ _____

   ➤ _____

3. Are the answers to the first two questions consistent or not? Why?

   _____

   _____

4. What is one major experience that had a profound influence on your life, and what life treasure did it leave you with?

   _____

   _____

5. Describe one event in which you touched the life of another person. (It can range from holding the hand of an ill person to saving a life. Don't restrict yourself to *your* perceived magnitude.)

   _____

   _____

6. What are three things you want others to say about you?

   ➤ _____

   ➤ _____

   ➤ _____

7. What has been your greatest accomplishment?

   _____

   _____

8. What project are you currently undertaking that elicits excitement from you?

   _____

   _____

Go back and review these questions and your responses. Put a star next to the two items that have the most meaning for you. Appreciate and acknowledge your accomplishments.

Nurture Noteworthy Networks

Television networks. Radio networks. Computer networks. Neural networks. All of these have sophisticated lines of transmission, whether through airwaves, optical fibers, or synaptic runways. Although their infrastructure varies, their goal is the same: to connect.

Often we regard the engineers and architects of network systems with awe and amazement. How do they do that? How do they design those convoluted connection contraptions?

Although these network notables deserve to be admired and applauded, you are really the ultimate network engineer. You can fabricate your own multilevel network system that will connect you to life.

To create a comprehensive network, you must give yourself permission to examine all aspects of your life: mind, body, spirit, and community. By nurturing a holistic network system, you exponentially increase your ability to touch the lives of others and be touched. Creating a network is about making a difference.

Network Notation

Noteworthy networks are those that have a notation greater than one. Too often we slip into the comfortable notion that one person can meet all our needs, support us, inspire us, enlighten us, warm us, love us, challenge us, and educate us. We need to expand our networks, which will in turn help us elevate the quality of life.

The easiest way to expand your network system is to seek out others. When you interact with other people, whether you are helping them or they are helping you, an incredibly powerful symbiotic relationship can be formed. Growth occurs for all parties involved.

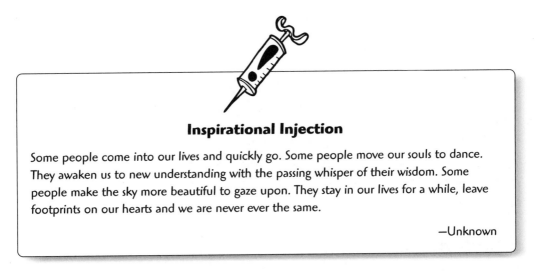

Inspirational Injection

Some people come into our lives and quickly go. Some people move our souls to dance. They awaken us to new understanding with the passing whisper of their wisdom. Some people make the sky more beautiful to gaze upon. They stay in our lives for a while, leave footprints on our hearts and we are never ever the same.

—Unknown

There is a caveat. Those involved in networks do not have to be friends. If friendship results, great—but in most networks, friendship is not a necessary factor. A relationship based upon mutual respect is all that is needed.

Ideas for Nourishing Networks

When you are open and receptive to network opportunities, then you yield profound personal growth. Look for network partners. Let others know what you are doing. You will discover an abundance of people who want to be part of your life. Listed below are some ideas for nourishing networks. Feel free to add your own.

Network Opportunities

1. Mind

➤ Intellectual:

Take a class.

Join a book club.

Visit a museum or an art gallery.

➤ **Emotional:**

Discover ways to control the stress in your life.

Seek outlets to foster emotional connections.

Actively pursue new friendships.

2. **Body**

Join a health club.

Walk regularly around your neighborhood.

Attend a nutrition seminar.

Visit a health food store.

3. **Spirit**

Get involved with a spiritual community.

Pray or meditate.

Clarify your values.

4. **Community**

Volunteer

Become involved with the PTA.

Help organize community clean-up efforts.

Cultivate career networks.

Reflection Quote

Happiness does not depend upon a full pocketbook, but upon a mind full of rich thoughts and a heart full of rich emotions.

—Wilfred Peterson

Reflection Quote

It takes as much courage to have tried and failed as to have tried and succeeded.

—Anne Morrow Lindbergh

There are several myths surrounding the idea of network. These include:

➤ Networks are only for career enhancement.

➤ Networks mean long-term relationships.

➤ Networks are more effective if they support your current ideas.

➤ Network-building just happens.

The network realities are that:

➤ Network relationships can last anywhere from a moment to a lifetime.

➤ You choose your networks.

➤ The more diverse your networks, the greater the chance for personal growth.

➤ The more open you are to self-growth, the more beneficial your networks will be.

178

➤ Network-negotiating is an active process.

➤ Letting people know your goals will only enlarge your network system.

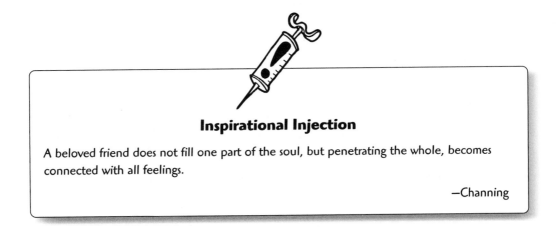

Inspirational Injection

A beloved friend does not fill one part of the soul, but penetrating the whole, becomes connected with all feelings.

—Channing

Interconnection Intricacies

The beauty of networks is that they are not limited by hierarchical structures. Rather, they are liberated by a lattice effect of interconnections. These interconnections are the substance and surprise of true living. Reflect back on conversations that ended with the line, "It sure is a small world." Events that evoke this response are the phenomena of interconnections personified. Although we may discover many of the interconnections serendipitously, we can and do birth many of the interconnections. The challenge is to use the interconnections for enlightenment, understanding, and fulfilled living.

Expose Yourself! (To Life Lessons, That Is)

Your life lessons have come when you have been exposed to something new, whether an encounter with a thought, an experience, or a person. This exposure may have been invited or it may have "just shown up." With this lesson, you also gained another puzzle piece of your life. You are different because of the learning.

By virtue of being human, you will be exposed to many learning situations—both good and bad. But what if you expose yourself to growth-producing situations by design? When you do so consciously, you enter the arena with openness and gain much from the experience.

With an open mind-set, a vulnerable mind-set, a student mind-set—the whole world opens its books

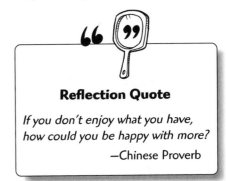

Reflection Quote

If you don't enjoy what you have, how could you be happy with more?

—Chinese Proverb

179

and shares with you knowledge and wisdom that will change your life. Learning is not just about receiving, but also about pursuing. Learning explorers find the paths that lead to optimal living. The trek need not be expensive, treacherous, or draining. The only cost is commitment. Here are some things you can consider, for starters:

➤ Go to the theater.

➤ Visit a natural wonder.

➤ Interview a centenarian.

➤ Read a novel by an author you've never read.

➤ Take a ride on the information highway.

➤ Play with some modeling clay.

➤ Attend a lecture on a topic you know very little about.

➤ Have a conversation with someone who is in a different philosophical camp than you are.

➤ Ask a child for a piece of advice.

➤ Go to the zoo and learn as much as you can about a specific animal.

Activities like these will give you new lenses with which to view the world. Experiences create who we are, and after new adventures we are never the same. That is the real beauty of being a unique, one-of-a-kind person.

The Least You Need to Know

➤ You are your greatest resource.

➤ The true treasures are within.

➤ You own the network.

➤ Be rare or be square.

Chapter 18

Profit from the Power of Parameters

In This Chapter

➤ What do parameters have to do with success?

➤ What is the parameter evolutionary process?

➤ What is parameter paralysis?

➤ What is the parameter paradox?

Parameters are guidelines to help people succeed. But who exactly are they for?:

➤ For kids only? *No!*

➤ For young adults only? *No!*

➤ For adults only? *No!*

➤ For lion tamers only? *No!*

The fact is that we all need parameters. And when we succeed at one level, we concurrently prepare ourselves for addressing the challenge of the next level. Parameters provide needed boundaries and guidelines within which to work, and reduce opportunities for being overwhelmed. Parameters can be a very positive aspect of promoting personal growth.

Fire insurance. Car insurance. Homeowner's insurance. These are all necessary and important types of insurance policies. However, they share a common denominator—they are reactive. These policies become valued only if something negative happens. We invest money hoping that something *won't* happen.

I'll bet you were wondering why I didn't mention life insurance in the preceding paragraph. It's because that's what this whole book is about—insuring that you have a more fulfilled life!

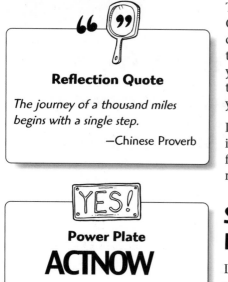

Reflection Quote

The journey of a thousand miles begins with a single step.

—Chinese Proverb

Power Plate

ACTNOW

There is another kind of insurance policy out there. Called a "Small Step to Success" insurance policy, it differs from other insurance policies in that it is proactive. It requires you to take action to create success in your life. You become the insurance agent actively taking control of your circumstances, your dreams, and your living.

Let's take a closer look at the "Small Steps to Success" insurance policy. The premise is that small steps toward focused dreams, tasks, and life endeavors yield great rewards.

Small Steps to Success Insurance Policy

Like all kinds of insurance policies, this one has terms and conditions, beneficiaries, and premiums.

Terms and Conditions

Term 1: Live—Minute to Minute. Enjoy the present moment. By becoming involved with the present you are able to enjoy the full fruits of living. The creation of your life is a moment-to-moment endeavor. It can be the smile of a child, the sound of a babbling brook, the salutation of the sunrise, or the glimmer in your friend's eye. Moments enrich our present and inform our future.

Term 2: Live—Day to Day. Day to day—this is the perspective piece that allows us to trek on. The old maxim, "one day at a time," encourages us to enjoy the day, to live in the now and not burden ourselves with the overwhelming worries of tomorrow. In fact, by living life to the fullest we invite tremendous tomorrows.

There is another reason to live the day to the fullest, which is that tomorrow may be very different from today. All you have to do is listen to the news or to your colleagues to hear about life-altering events. Tomorrow you may not have the chance to say "I love you" to someone. You may not have the chance to say "Thanks for making a difference in my life." You may not have the chance to give the consoling comfort of a hug. Today is the day to do these things. You may not get another chance.

Reflection Quote

The only way to move a mountain is one shovel at time.

—Unknown

Term three: Live—Year to Year. Yearly reflections can help catapult you into a successful future. Too often we look back and say, "What if?" or "Why didn't I?" You can use reflections for a refreshing renewal of yourself. Reinvigorate yourself with the *Re*-vival formula:

➤ *Re*-energize. Human beings are forces of energy excited by the collaborative efforts of the mind, body, and spirit. When you seek to harmonize these aspects of your life, you find a wellspring of energy that enables you to accomplish whatever you truly desire. The energy will come forth to make your dreams come true.

➤ *Re*-commit. Recommit to your own dreams and goals. Transform the ethereal notions and ideas into concrete steps of action. By recommitting to your dreams, you are recommitting to yourself. Next time you undergo your yearly reflection, you'll be able to say, "Here are the steps I took and this is what I accomplished."

➤ *Re*-create. Through recreation you inject properties of wholeness, fun, and enthusiasm. You stimulate the unseen qualities of fulfilled living. You also bring that childlike wonder and excitement to your being. Recreation must be incorporated into your life plan.

Reflection Quote

What I'm doing today is important because I'm exchanging a day of my life for it.

—Hugh Mulligan

➤ *Re*-minisce. Reminiscing on the adventures of the past year can be very powerful. Some adventures may have been pleasant, some not. However, the paths you took and the terrain you traversed presented life lessons that, if acknowledged, enhance the essence of who you are.

Inspirational Injection

Don't be fooled by the calendar. There are only as many days in the year as we make use of. One person gets only a week's value of a year, while another person gets a full year's value out of a week.

—Charles Richards

Dual Beneficiaries

The great part is that this insurance policy promotes opportunities for dual beneficiaries. The beneficiaries are (1) *you* and (2) society.

Reflection Quote

If you carry your childhood with you, you never become older.

—Abraham Sutzkever

Unconventional Wisdom

Everyone has talent. What is rare is the courage to follow the talent to the dark places where it leads.

—Erica Jong

➤ *You!* You are the primary beneficiary because you are actively changing your life. You learn from both the bumps and the joys. The more you participate in life-fulfilling activities, the more benefits you will receive. Small steps enable you to build skills and confidence, which yield success. You also benefit in another way. The victories you enjoy enable you to take bigger steps and more advanced challenges that enlarge your personhood. *Step on!*

➤ Society. Our society works because of individuals. It is not a system, or a group, or a process—certainly these are all factors, but none of them exist without individuals bringing their talents and abilities to the table. When the collective abilities of individuals are combined for the common good, then society as a whole benefits. You have something special to offer to society, and we will all be the beneficiaries. Let your individual light shine and join it with others. Together you can illuminate the world!

Premiums

The amount and frequency of payments are not fixed, but rather are highly variable. Both are determined by the specific task at hand. You pay sometimes hourly, daily, weekly, monthly, yearly and "lifely" (how's that for a word!). Payment changes according to the life issue and its magnitude.

The currency used for payment might be time, emotion, knowledge, or laughter. It changes with the scenario. The cost can range from minimal to expensive.

The other facet has to do with co-payments. Much of what we do to fulfill our dreams requires a co-payment structure. In fact, co-payment is the norm. Seldom can we realize our dreams without the help and assistance of others. They pay—they invest in us. This interdependency is what provides the greatest riches for us and for our society. Oh, don't forget to send your co-payee a thank you for his or her generous payment.

Shoe Size: Not a Factor

When you take your steps to success, the size of your shoes doesn't matter. Folks with gigantic feet are no more successful than folks with tiny feet. What will determine your success is the size of your heart, the power of your dream, and your commitment to succeed—all combined with the steps to make it happen. This mix of ingredients is the recipe for earning success in your life.

Parameter Evolution: Enlarge Your Life

Evolution. It's everywhere—even in the parameter world. An enlarged life is created when we succeed at the progressive levels of evolution. The following example illustrates this concept.

You have set a goal to run a marathon. It's a pretty ambitious goal, complete with blisters and sweat. Even more ambitious when you aren't even a runner yet!

So do you sign up for the marathon and go run without practice or preparation? Of course not. If you did, what would be the result? Failure and probably injury. You need some parameters to help make you successful.

In fact, you'll need to be a partner in the parameter-evolution process. I'll walk you through this example. I guess we should *run* through the example, but let's start off slowly.

Here are the steps:

1. Learn to walk, and then to run.

2. Run around the block.

3. Read about marathon preparation.

4. Run one mile.

5. Run five miles.

6. Get your head examined!

7. Run some road races, maybe some 10 K's.

8. Buy some new shoes.

9. Wash your socks once a year, whether they need it or not.

10. Boost mileage to 10 miles.

11. Run a half-marathon.

12. Buy high-tech equipment and spend lots of money.

13. Start looking for a marathon to run—choose the flattest course possible.

14. Sign up, and continue to follow the training manual.

15. Run the marathon, buy the shirt, and tell everyone you have ever met in your entire life.

Reflection Quote

There is only one success—to be able to spend your life in your own way.

—Morley

Each of these steps involves parameters. You're successful when you accomplish the task at each level. You accomplish the task by mastering the skills and taking action. Once you're successful, you can expand the parameter base to allow greater opportunities.

If there are no parameters established, then you don't know where to begin and you set yourself up for failure. You don't know what limits you should respect. In this example, as in many instances, the steps are cumulative—they build on one another. Success comes from step-building.

Smaller-Larger-Smaller Phenomenon

There is an interesting phenomenon in parameter paradise. It's called the smaller-larger-smaller phenomenon. This is how it works. As you enjoy success at a lower (smaller) level in the evolutionary scheme, you then get to move to a larger level of parameters. Then what happens is that the larger level which you now inhabit becomes the smaller. You seek success at this level so that you can move to the next larger level, which will shortly be the smaller level. The process continues.

At first glance you might say, "If this is true, are you really getting anywhere if your largers become your smallers?" The best way to look at this is from a longer view, from a perspective that allows you to look at a larger segment of your life. Compare where you were when you started this book with where you are now. That's when you see the value of parameter evolution and its link to dramatic growth.

Unconventional Wisdom

Argue for your limitations and sure enough they're yours.

—Richard Bach

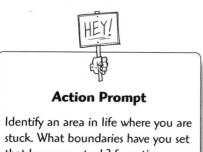

Action Prompt

Identify an area in life where you are stuck. What boundaries have you set that keep you stuck? Sometimes we get stuck because our parameters are too tight. Redefine what you want to accomplish and create two goals you can tackle this week to give you the jump start you need. Now—*follow through!*

Beware of Parameter Paralysis

One extreme of the world of parameters results in an insidious disease called parameter paralysis. This disease infiltrates the decision-making marrow. Those infected conjure up elaborate limitations and rules that obstruct the ability to move beyond the confines of the preset parameters.

So you might be thinking, "But Mark, I don't understand. You said that parameters were important for living." Yes, parameters are important, but they are to serve only as guidelines for living. If they restrict us too much, then we strangle. Parameters are designed to be guidelines for growth, not inhibitors of growth.

1. How do you let parameters paralyze you?

_____

_____

2. How do you use parameters to foster personal growth?

_____

_____

3. What is one thing you could do to profit from parameters?

_____

_____

Inspirational Injection

The Station

Tucked away in our subconscious is an idyllic vision. We see ourselves on a long trip that spans the continent. We are traveling by train.

Out the windows we drink in the passing scene of cars on nearby highways, of children waving at a crossing, of cattle grazing on a distant hillside, of smoke pouring from a power plant, of row upon row of corn and wheat, of flatlands and valleys, of mountains and rolling hillsides, of city skylines and village halls.

But uppermost in our minds is the final destination. Bands will be playing and flags waving. Once we get there our dreams will come true, and the pieces of our lives will fit together like a jigsaw puzzle. How restlessly we pace the aisles, damning the minutes for loitering—waiting, waiting, waiting for the station.

"When we reach the station, that will be it!" we cry.

"When I'm 18."

"When I buy a new 450SL Mercedes-Benz!"

"When I put the last kid through college."

"When I have paid off the mortgage."

"When I get a promotion."

"When I reach the age of retirement, I shall live happily ever after."

Sooner or later we must realize there is no station, no one place to arrive at once and for all. The true joy of life is the trip. The station is only a dream and outdistances us.

—Robert J. Hastings

Parameter Paradox

Boundaries, limits, rules, guidelines…are all words associated with parameters.

Look at this title: "Parameter Evolution: Enlarge Your Life." How can the words *parameter* and *enlarge* reside in the same sentence? They definitely seem contradictory. When you think of the word "parameter," you go back to that boundary and limitation type of thinking. Then there is that word "enlarge," which connotes ideas like *expansion* and *flexibility*.

Help! We need to reconcile this.

This is the parameter paradox. The paradox actually makes a lot of sense. What happens is that we start off with a given set of parameters. We learn to become successful within those parameters. Then the base enlarges and we become proficient in the next arena, and so on. The residual effect is growth. Your world gets enlarged and the growth stimulates additional growth—a wonderful cycle of development.

Power Plate

BSUCSFL

Human beings need parameters. The challenge is to use them, not to let them use you.

The Least You Need To Know

➤ Parameters can help you be successful.

➤ The key agent to insure your success is *you*.

➤ You can avoid parameter paralysis—open your mind today.

➤ Parameters can excite growth; don't let them inhibit.

Part 7

Communication:
Stop, Look, Listen, Grow!

Oratory leaves a smokescreen;
eloquence, a vapor trail;
sincerity, an endowment.

—Thomas S. Silver

Each of us communicates with others every day—at some level. But how satisfactory are those communications? Do real ideas get conveyed, or is it just words bandied back and forth? To build up your communications skills, you'll learn first of all to communicate with yourself, practicing perpetual affirmations and acknowledging when you make steps (even small steps) forward. Then you can focus on listening to others—not only hearing the words, but hearing at a deeper level and asking the right questions to learn more. You'll also expand your awareness of nonverbal communication—touch.

GO, ME, GO!

Chapter 19

Enthuse Yourself

In This Chapter

➤ How to enthuse yourself

➤ How to use the power of self-talk

➤ How to profit from perpetual affirmations

➤ How to combat perfectionism

There really was a fifth main character in the movie *The Wizard of Oz*. You didn't know that, did you? He was a rooster. When he woke up in the morning, he was not enthusiastic about greeting the day with a good ol' cock-a-doodle-do. In fact, he wasn't enthusiastic about anything. Dorothy, the Cowardly Lion, the Scarecrow, and the Tin Man tried to talk him into coming with them to Oz to see the Wizard, but he just couldn't get excited about the trip. He had asked rooster elder after rooster elder where he could obtain the gift of enthusiasm. Unfortunately, none of them had the answer. He was exhausted from his search. His enthusiasm was gone and he made the decision to stay where he was.

After Dorothy and her friends discovered that home, courage, intellect, and love could not be given by anyone else—that these qualities come from within—they realized that this was also true for enthusiasm. They used their Ozular phone to call their unenthusiastic rooster friend, and explained that he already had his enthusiasm—he just had to tap it. The enthusiasm program is in the brain; it only has to be stimulated. Once the rooster heard that he already had the "gift," he began cock-a-doodle-doing as he never had done before. He found it.

Wouldn't it be great if it were that simple? But it's not. We know that no one else can make you enthusiastic. You have to do it yourself. It takes work, but most of all it takes doing things that are important to you, doing things that you believe in.

Power Plate

GTXCITD

Enthusiasm does have some incredible properties when we consciously tap it. It's a catalyst for excellence. It's like the elixir used to change lead to gold (I always wanted to learn how to do that). Enthusiasm is the ingredient that enables a person to leave the abyss of mediocrity and discover the higher order of existence called optimal living.

Let's get enthused!

Inspirational Injection

If you can't get enthused about your work, its time to get alarmed—something is wrong. Compete with yourself: grit your teeth and dive into the job of breaking your own record. No one keeps up enthusiasm automatically. Enthusiasm must be nourished with new actions, new aspirations, new efforts, new vision. If you want to turn hours into minutes, renew your enthusiasm.

—Papyrus

Self-Talk: Yes, You Are Listening

It's morning. You get your cup of coffee or diet cola, walk over to your computer, and turn it on to check your e-mail. The first message you see on the screen asks, "What is your password?" You type **CARPEDIEM**. Think about what you have just done. You told yourself to seize the day—and it was one of the first messages you received. When you say to yourself *seize the day* it definitely sets a tone. It proactively propels your thoughts in positive directions and sets the course for action.

All this from a password? When I first started using passwords, they were definitely vanity plate–type messages. My philosophy regarding passwords has changed drastically during the past several years. I now use them as a jump start for positive and productive thinking. Passwords like carpediem, seizeit, success, goforit, and care4all all help to focus my mind and actions on what is important. Hmm. The real goal of passwords—to open computer applications? *No.* Rather, to open perspectives and set a positive foundation for the day. I won't complain about passwords any more.

Passwords—a form of self-talk. Definitely.

Action Prompt

Change your passwords today!

5,413,243,612 Gazillion

"What is that number?" you ask. Well, last I counted, it was the number of words a person says to her- or himself during a two-week period. The number might not be totally accurate, and if you are not comfortable with it then I'll let you count, if you want.

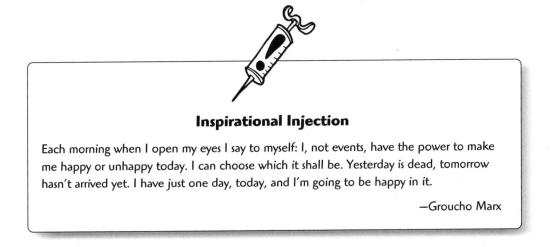

Inspirational Injection

Each morning when I open my eyes I say to myself: I, not events, have the power to make me happy or unhappy today. I can choose which it shall be. Yesterday is dead, tomorrow hasn't arrived yet. I have just one day, today, and I'm going to be happy in it.

—Groucho Marx

Think about it. When you get up in the morning, who is the very first person you talk to? Who is the last person you talk to before going to bed? Who is the person you talk to most between sunup and sundown? *You!* Usually, we don't think about communication this way.

Well, if you talk to yourself all day, every day of your life, think of the enormous power in the words you say to yourself. There is a definite influence, and the choice is yours whether to control the messages that reach your inner ear, your mind, your soul, and your heart. Yes, you do have that imperative.

So you say, "Fine, but how do I influence myself through words?" First you need to examine yourself through objective lenses (one size does *not* fit

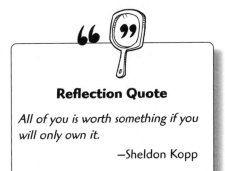

Reflection Quote

All of you is worth something if you will only own it.

—Sheldon Kopp

all). You need to evaluate how much of your self-talk is negative and how much is positive. I can listen to you and tell you how much I hear that is positive and negative, but I hear only the smallest fraction of what you say compared to what you hear.

Answer honestly the questions in this self-talk inventory:

1. What do I say when I look in the mirror?

   Examples: "Gee I'm looking fine today," or "I sure am looking old."

   _____

2. What do I say when I have to run a meeting?

   Examples: "I will have their rapt attention," or "I'm afraid they won't even listen to me."

   _____

3. What do I say when I have to attend a social function?

   Examples: "People will like my sense of humor," or "No one will even want to talk with me."

   _____

Are you on the positive side or the negative side of the continuum? Reframe the answers so that you can start scooting to the positive side.

POSITIVE <————————————————————————————————> NEGATIVE

Common Replies to Salutations

What are the common phrases you use all day long? How do you respond when someone asks, "How are you?"

➤ "I'm surviving."

➤ "I can't complain, and no one would listen if I did."

➤ "I'm holding on until Friday."

➤ "Just putting in my eight."

➤ "I'm alive; it beats the alternative."

What are the actual phrases you use?

_____

_____

Now multiply the number of people you greet each day times the response you give, and the product will be the message you really give yourself—not others. As you reinforce this message, it becomes a more solid image and strengthens its impact on your life.

If your responses are positive, great. You can pass Go and collect your money. If they are negative, then stay with me for a minute.

Okay. What are some positive phrases you can try? Here are some examples:

➤ I'm doing great.

➤ Life is going well.

➤ I'm having fun.

Create some that you can try:

Reflection Quote

When you expect the best, you release a magnetic force in your mind, which by the law of attraction brings the best to you.

—Norman Vincent Peale

_____

_____

_____

Jettison the "I Grew Up That Way" Excuse

I'm the way I am because I grew up that way. Or I was always told I was stupid and worthless, and that I couldn't do anything right." Have you ever heard someone say that? Have *you* ever said that?

Ready, set—jettison this excuse and this type of thinking. Certainly your past experiences influence your personhood, and it's not uncommon to find yourself repeating the messages that you heard over and over again growing up. If they were positive messages, great— but often they were negative. You do not need to be a victim paralyzed by the negative programs established during your childhood.

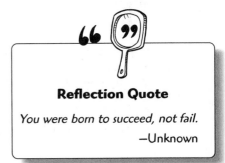

Reflection Quote

You were born to succeed, not fail.

—Unknown

Now is the time to change the program. You can create your own Independence Day. You have from this moment until you die to make life a positive ride and a rich adventure. By incorporating positive self-talk and taking positive action, you begin the rewarding journey.

Create a Great Day

Author Dan Millman shares the phrase "Create a nice day." Talk about incredible messages. This one short salutation is packed with power. With gratitude to Millman

195

for the phrase, I would like to change one word, so that the phrase reads, "Create a great day. Let's look a little bit closer at the phrase. "Create" means that you are in the driver's seat—you have the control. "Great" means above the norm, better than average. What if you said "Create a mediocre day"? Not very powerful, is it? It is only one step above, "Have a nice day," a passive expression that sounds as though you give the other person permission to surrender all control for the outcome of the day.

Let's take an even deeper look at the phrase. When you say, "Create a great day" to another person, you're really sending two messages—one to the other person and one to yourself. (You were wondering how I was going to get around to self-talk, weren't you?) Every time you say this phrase to someone, it serves as a reinforcement for self-injection of the notion. It's a stimulus for you to do the same.

Power Plate

CR8GRT1

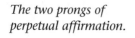

Unconventional Wisdom

Positive thinking reaps the greatest reward when it is married to positive action.

The receiver of the message also takes notice. Since it's not a generic phrase, it piques the interest of the other person, nudging his or her mind and actually making the person think about your words. You become a catalyst of change, helping others to look at their day differently.

With gratitude to the original author of this phrase, I've adopted it and use it in my daily dealings with others. My voice-mail message ends with "create a great day." It always catches folk by surprise, and at least one-fourth of the callers acknowledge the unusual salutation (and always in a positive way). I also use it when I finish a conversation with someone. I continue its use because I have personally witnessed its power.

Try it out. See how it works for you.

Practice Perpetual Affirmations

Affirm thyself—again and again and again. You can have a dramatic impact on the quality of your day by practicing perpetual affirmations. You might ask, "What in the world is a perpetual affirmation?" Actually, it's a two-pronged endeavor that you can do more effectively than anyone else.

The two prongs of perpetual affirmation.

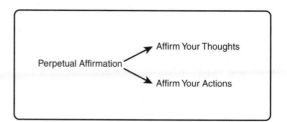

Affirm Your Thoughts

Self-help writers have discussed this notion of self-affirmation for years. When you take all the wisdom from those thinkers and distill it into one definition, affirming your thoughts simply means telling yourself something you want to become true. The theory is that by repeatedly telling yourself something, your actions change to make the words true. For example, if day after day I say that I'm a creative person, then I begin to believe it, I take actions to make it true, I reinforce that I am creative, and through the magic of perpetuality—voilá— I'm a creative person.

The first step in affirming thoughts is to decide what you want to become. What do you believe in? What are your goals? Often the affirming thoughts center around your mission or purpose in life.

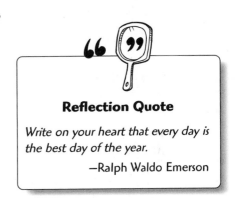

After you figure out the "what," you need to look at the "when." The timing of thought affirmations is critical. In fact, with strategic timing you can create a compound effect. By committing to a specific time each day for this activity, you put the behavior into operation and make it routine, creating a positive habit as part of your daily routine. The two key times are first thing in the morning and last thing at night.

Reflection Quote

Write on your heart that every day is the best day of the year.

—Ralph Waldo Emerson

Morning Affirmation

You may have heard this old adage: "Some people wake up in the morning and say, 'Good God, it's morning,' and others wake up and say, 'Good morning, God'." What is your approach to the day?

The way you frame your thoughts at the beginning of the day will have a tremendous impact on the way your day turns out. By focusing your thoughts on positive self-image and outcomes for the day, you acknowledge the importance of your own personhood while at the same time mobilizing your energies in a positive direction. This process allows you to center yourself and think about things that are *really* important. It also helps you keep the bumps in life in perspective.

A very important part of the self-affirmation process is to have this talk with yourself before you do anything else. Well, you can visit the bathroom and the coffee pot, but don't dare touch a TV, radio, or newspaper. This talk allows your thoughts to be formed without being bombarded by external stimuli—most of which will probably be negative.

Action Prompt

Create your own set of affirmations, tailored to enhance your uniqueness.

Here is an actual example of what I read every day for my morning affirmation:

The Prayer of Saint Francis

Lord make me an instrument of your peace.

Where there is hatred, let me sow love.

Where there is injury, pardon.

Where there is doubt, faith.

Where there is despair, hope.

Where there is darkness, light.

Where there is sadness, joy.

Where there is discord, unity.

Where there is error, truth.

O Divine Master, grant that I may not so
much seek to be consoled, as to console;
to be understood, as to understand;
to be loved as to love; for it is in giving
that we receive; it is in pardoning that we
are pardoned; and it is in dying that we are
born to eternal life.

1. I make a difference.
2. I will enrich my mind:
   ➤ Intellectually
   ➤ Emotionally

3. I will enrich my spirit:
   ➤ Worship God.
   ➤ Establish life purpose.

4. I will enrich my body:

> ➤ Exercise three times a week.

> ➤ Eat well.

5. I will be a good husband and father:

> ➤ Spend time with my wife.

> ➤ Spend time with my daughters.

6. I will be a mentor to others.

7. I will serve others.

8. I will enrich my community.

9. I am a person of integrity.

This affirmation gives me my charge for the day, helping me center and focus on the important things in my life.

The process of initializing your day with positive thought that requires action will enhance the quality of your life. Combining this with the power of a daily ritual strengthens the message and helps you create the *you* you want to become.

YES!

Power Plate

ICANDO

Unconventional Wisdom

You are never given a wish without also being given the power to make it true. You may have to work for it, however.

—Richard Bach

Night Affirmations

There is a special time between getting into bed and falling asleep (watch your minds). If you take just a couple of minutes to reflect on your day, you can create some magic in your life. Reflect on the positive things that happened. What did you accomplish? What were the highlights? What might you do differently tomorrow? What are you thankful for? If you can't answer these questions, then you are not thinking hard enough. Give it another shot. This type of reflection provides closure to the day and yields a sense of peace that will result in a much more restful night. And if you wish, add one or two night affirmations to your reflections before you drift off to sleep. Before reading any further, try to come up with a few affirmations of your own.

Misplaced Focus Syndrome Vaccination

You might ask, "Why all of the emphasis on the positive aspect of our lives?" The answer is simple, yet profound. The positive approach to living serves as the vaccination to prevent the Misplaced Focus Syndrome (MFS), which is the disease of negativism. The MFS is one that we all catch at some point in our lives. Do you remember a day when many positive things and maybe one negative thing happened to you? Did you focus on the one negative thing and disregard all the positive events?

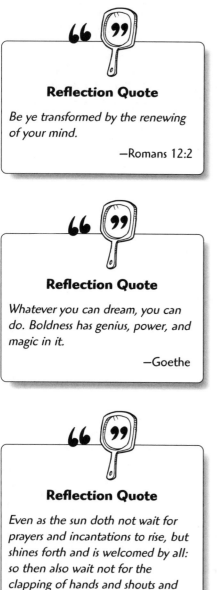

Reflection Quote

Be ye transformed by the renewing of your mind.

—Romans 12:2

Reflection Quote

Whatever you can dream, you can do. Boldness has genius, power, and magic in it.

—Goethe

Reflection Quote

Even as the sun doth not wait for prayers and incantations to rise, but shines forth and is welcomed by all: so then also wait not for the clapping of hands and shouts and praise to do thy duty; nay, do good of thine own accord, and thou wilt be loved like the sun.

—Epictetus

The vaccination for the MFS is unlike other vaccinations. Many vaccinations are one-shot deals (okay, so the pun was intended), but the MFS vaccination needs to be injected every single day—by *you*. It costs less money than any other vaccination you will ever get, but is it expensive in that it takes an investment of your time. The investment will yield a multitude of life fruits, however.

Affirm Your Actions

Affirming your actions is a different endeavor than affirming your thoughts. Rather than having a morning and night focus, affirming your actions is an all-day activity. It's fairly easy, yet it can have potent effects. This is how you can do it. Let's say you're in the middle of your day and you're getting ready to meet with your boss. You decide to take a little extra initiative to give the boss more than she requested. After you present her with the information, you see that she is delighted you made the extra effort. At this point it is time to inject yourself with an action affirmation. Say to yourself, "Great job! The effort was worth it. Way to go." That's an active affirmation. It's that easy. Simple yet effective.

Action affirmations can be used for small or large actions—the key is that you acknowledge the action. *Note:* You do not need to tell anyone else you did a great job. This is your personal recognition. Your triumph is internal.

Recognize Successive Approximations, *not* Perfection

A hundred years ago, when I was taking a psychology class in college, my wise professor was talking about the concept of rewarding successive approximations. With eyes glazed, I half-ear-edly listened, knowing that I would never use this stuff. It would never be relevant to my life. (Have you ever said that when you were taking a class?) Boy, was I wrong!

Simply put, successive approximations relate to behavior. If you want someone to exhibit a certain behavior, break it down into components that build upon one another—called *successive approximations of the task*. After the person is successful at implementing the first component of the behavior, you recognize and reward the behavior. Then, on completion of the second component of the behavior, you reward that behavior, and so on until the entire behavior is exhibited. The rewards along the way serve as reinforcers and encouragers.

Now apply this concept to yourself. Break your tasks into components. As you become proficient or accomplish a component, reward yourself. Become your own cheerleader.

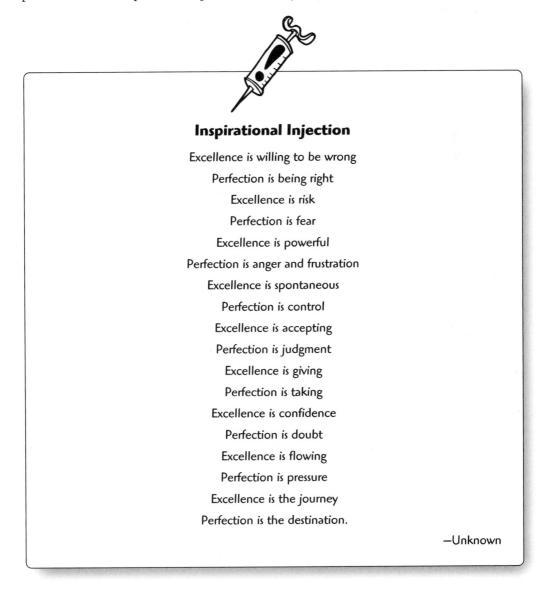

Inspirational Injection

Excellence is willing to be wrong

Perfection is being right

Excellence is risk

Perfection is fear

Excellence is powerful

Perfection is anger and frustration

Excellence is spontaneous

Perfection is control

Excellence is accepting

Perfection is judgment

Excellence is giving

Perfection is taking

Excellence is confidence

Perfection is doubt

Excellence is flowing

Perfection is pressure

Excellence is the journey

Perfection is the destination.

—Unknown

Unconventional Wisdom

The only thing you can do perfectly is to be imperfect.

The opposite of rewarding successive approximations is a little life detractor called *perfectionism.* "If I can't do it perfectly the first time, then I'm a failure." Sound familiar? Perfectionism is the enemy of growth. Give yourself a break—please. No one is perfect, and no one will ever be, thank heavens. Once you give yourself permission to accept that fact, you will enjoy your life a lot more.

Practice rewarding yourself, using the concept of recognizing successive approximations. You will find that the tasks become more manageable and fulfilling.

The Least You Need to Know

➤ You are responsible for your own enthusiasm.

➤ Your internal message system creates who you are.

➤ Affirm yourself—don't wait for others to do it.

➤ Use the magic of successive approximations to promote self-growth.

Chapter 20

Listen, Listen, Listen— or Misunderstand

In This Chapter

➤ How to reprogram your brain

➤ How to use your blinders

➤ How to expand your small-talk repertoire

➤ How to ask one more question

Some people have big ones. Some have pointy ones. Some have hairy ones, but everyone has them. No, not heads—*ears!* Actually, when you look at an ear, it's a pretty funny-looking contraption. The ultimate architect designed it so that this funnel-type thing would catch sound. The sound catcher is attached to a tunnel lined with cilia (a nicer word than hair), and the tunnel is attached to a drum. I always wondered where they found someone small enough to get in there and play that thing.

Now that's the interior part of the ear. Think about the external dressings. Some individuals grow their hair long to keep their ears a secret, while others use them for jewelry hangers to draw attention to them. The latter group of people are called ear exhibitionists.

Unconventional Wisdom

You can only truly listen by living in the present.

Power Plate

YES!

I HEAR U

Action Prompt

HEY!

Next time you have a conversation with someone, practice these two cardinal rules:

1. Don't interrupt the other person.

2. Don't finish the other person's sentences.

But no matter what the shape, the decorations, or the attractiveness—the ear serves one essential purpose: to listen. The fallacy is that just because we have the physical mechanisms as part of the infrastructure, we listen. Wrong. Even with the proper equipment, the person owning those ears does not necessarily listen.

Engage Ears Before Mouth

I remember years ago a wise mother telling me, "My son is not hard of hearing, he's hard of listening." Sometimes the wire in our head between hearing and listening gets disconnected. The sound may be audible, but the understanding is absent.

Unfortunately, another problem occurs. For many people the first sound of a word that hits their ear results in two reflex actions: listening stops, and the mouth engages. Yes, someone else's words act as a stimulus for your mouth (evidence of the first use of wireless in communication).

The big question is how many words hit your eardrum before your mouth starts: 2, 6, 15? The lower the number, the more you need to pay attention to the following sections. If you have a high words-to-eardrum ratio, you may skip the next section. In fact, why don't you treat your ears to some soothing music.

We've already looked at one problem regarding listening—the word-to-eardrum ratio. Let's take it a step further. It's possible to have a high word-to-eardrum ratio without truly listening.

The listening process can be hindered by not using your gray matter between the reception of the sound and the movement of your mouth. Believe it or not, the brain is critical in the listening process. It's the component that helps you understand what the other person is saying and helps you form a response based on the message that was sent.

Sometime during our lives, our brains lost the program for true listening. Let's reload the program now. You can use the following commands:

1. Turn on brain.

2. Receive sounds through ears.

3. Use brain (a key step many of us forget).

204

4. Form response.

5. Set mouth in motion.

6. Repeat.

Program your brain so that this set of commands occurs in a continuous loop. And be sure to employ steps 3 and 4. Now instead of being hard of listening, you will be easy of listening.

Put On Blinders and Focus

Imagine this scene. Tiger Woods, the golf phenom, walks up to the eighteenth green to a cheering throng of onlookers who are witnessing one of the finest exhibitions in golf history. This was the 1997 Masters. Tiger Woods had one of the biggest leads of all time and was getting ready to enjoy a 12-stroke triumph.

Once Tiger got to his ball on the green, the crowd hushed. Tiger had a new trademark, not one worn on clothes, but rather an action he used to focus. To site his putt, Tiger bent his knees, rested on his haunches, and put his hands on either side of his head, holding on to the bill of his golf cap. He was creating his own set of blinders. This action enabled him to minimize outside distractions and promote his ability to focus. Young Tiger Woods knew that if he was going to succeed, he had to take proactive measures to help him focus—he consciously put on his blinders. That day, the youngest Master's champion changed the look of golf forever. Worldwide, golfers of all ages began using the Tiger Blinders Technique. A new tradition for golf was created that day.

When it comes to listening, we can learn a lesson from Tiger (he and I are not really on a first-name basis, but it sounds better). We consciously have to put on blinders so that we can focus more effectively on what is being said by the person with whom we are conversing. Now I don't recommend the Tiger Blinders Technique while you're talking with someone else; you might scare them. But I do urge that you find other ways to focus.

The key to focusing is to make a conscious effort to give your undivided attention. Giving undivided attention sounds easy, doesn't it? Here is a news bulletin: *it's not!* Think of some times when you were the victim of divided attention:

➤ The time you were having a conversation with someone and the other person kept answering the phone and conversing with those who called—while you were sitting there.

Reflection Quote

Concentrate all your thoughts upon the work at hand. The sun's rays do not burn until brought to a focus.

—Alexander Graham Bell

➤ The time you were talking with someone and the whole time you were speaking, the other person was looking around and behind you to see who might be coming.

➤ The time you were sitting across the table trying to communicate with your significant other and the only responses you received were some grunts, coming from behind the newspaper masking the person's face.

Unconventional Wisdom

Besides skill, what do you want most from your surgeon? Yes—undivided attention. In the middle of an operation, you don't want her or him watching a sit-com, eating lunch, or talking on the phone. So it is with communication.

Now, how did these interactions make you feel? I can make some guesses. "I'm not worthy," "You don't care about me," "I'm wasting your time." Unfortunately, divided attention exchanges can make you feel not so great about yourself. But the reality is this. You shouldn't be the one feeling bad. The other person should—for she or he is the one not listening, not paying attention, not giving you the respect you deserve.

Well, you don't want to be like others giving divided attention, so you might have to do a little introspection yourself. Do you give your undivided attention? Do you really listen? Remember those people who didn't give you their undivided attention? They didn't say to themselves "I'm purposefully *not* going to listen to so-and-so." They just weren't thinking. You can't change their behavior, but you can change your own behavior. Don't you get caught in the divided-attention trap.

Get Up Close and Personal (Not That Close)

As mentioned earlier in this book, many years ago I ran across the idea "Talk with a person as if it is the last conversation you will ever have with them." If followed, this nugget of wisdom would definitely enhance the depth and meaning of conversations.

Reflection Quote

When you stop learning, stop listening, stop looking, and asking questions, always new questions, that is the time to die.

—Lillian Smith

So you might be thinking: that sounds all well and good, but I don't have time in my life for conversations like that. It's not realistic and I'm too busy! Oh yes—the ubiquitous "I'm too busy" excuse which we conveniently invoke whenever we might have to invest part of ourselves. It's a lot easier to engage in unmeaningful superficial dialogue: "Yes, the weather is nice today," "Are you ready for the holidays?" and "I'll bet this is a busy time of the year for you."

We need to get back to person-to-person, heart-to-heart, soul-to-soul. True discovery of another comes through listening, empathizing, and focusing—through truly being there.

Expand Your Small Talk Repertoire

Picture in your mind the small talk soiree—or cocktail party—or a holiday business fete. You know the ritual. You walk up to someone and the small talk begins. Let's see. What will you talk about—weather, kids, work? And after you make small talk with seven different people and ask each of them the same set of questions, you are probably ready to go home. When you get home, you may be enriched by the finger foods, but not by the conversation.

I urge you to take the Expand Your Small Talk Challenge. Come up with a new list of party questions. Here are some to get you started:

➤ After finding out where the other person grew up, ask "What is your favorite childhood memory?"

➤ After asking about where the other person took a vacation, ask "If you were stranded on a deserted island for one year, and you could have only one other person with you (no significant other or children or friends), who would you choose?"

➤ After asking about holiday plans, ask "Where do you feel most at peace?"

These are just a few to stimulate your synapses. What others can you come up with? By taking a different approach to party talk, you will be the talk of the party. People will see you as a person of substance and you will definitely learn more about yourself and others. Enjoy the party.

Increase Your Reflection Power

Every communication, counseling, and interpersonal skills class has a requisite component regarding reflecting what you heard. Look Mom, no mirrors needed. To be an effective listener, you need to let the other person know you are really hearing her or him. The easiest way to do this is by reflecting back the content and feeling you heard expressed. When the other person hears your reflection, he or she thinks, *"You did listen to what I was saying."*

The most common phrase used in all those communications texts out there is, "I hear you saying...." Listen to this: *do not* say, "I hear you saying...." The minute you utter that phrase, the other person will quietly—or not so quietly—mutter under her or his breath, "Oh yeah, you just finished a listening course and that's what you were instructed to say." Don't be accused of being mechanical when your real goal is to be personal. You need to find your own way to reflect back; find

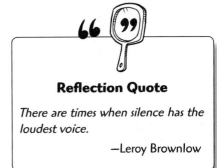

Reflection Quote

There are times when silence has the loudest voice.

—Leroy Brownlow

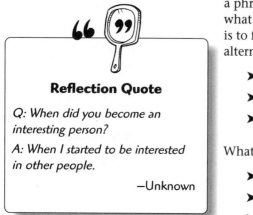

a phrase that's natural for you. You need to discover what fits you best, and the only way to effectively reflect is to focus on what is really being said. Here are some alternative reflection phrases:

➤ So you're saying…

➤ Let me see if I have this right…

➤ OK, I'm hearing that…

What are some other lines you could use?

➤

➤

➤

Ask Another Question

Picture this: you're sitting in the front passenger seat of your car. The view from this seat feels strange since you usually sit directly behind the steering wheel. Suddenly you glance to your left and see your 15-year-old son behind the wheel—grinning from ear to ear. He doesn't look a day over 12. Just this morning he got his learner's permit. You're sitting in a vacant parking lot, as far from civilization as you can possibly get. You've given him the preliminary instructions and he's ready to drive (*Help!*). He turns on the ignition, presses on the gas pedal, violently pops the clutch, and sends you and two tons of steel heading for a snow bank. Mother Nature saves you this time by placing a snow bank where you needed to stop. After making sure that each of you is okay, you ask in your calmest voice, *"Why didn't you step on the brake?"* He responds as if you're from another planet. "Oh, I forgot where it was. I was going to ask you later. Is it the pedal between the clutch and the gas?"

Wouldn't it have been nice if the boy in the car scenario had asked another question before he started the car moving? And preferably that question would have been, "Where is the brake?"

Likewise, we need to give ourselves the permission *and the responsibility* to ask another question. Before we look at the whys and hows of asking another question, let's look at the anatomy of following instructions.

The anatomy people most commonly use goes something like this:

➤ Hear instructions.

➤ Say "okay."

➤ Begin to implement plan.

Sounds familiar, doesn't it? The problem is that important parts of the anatomy are missing. By using the truncated version, you invite disaster and misunderstanding, although at first glance you appear to honor expediency.

Let me suggest a different anatomical structure. The one with all the trunks:

1. Hear instructions.
2. Reflect back.
3. Create a quick plan.
4. Ask another question.
5. Say "okay."
6. Begin to implement plan.

Power Plate

ILSTN2U

Since we're talking about anatomy, let's dissect this formula:

1. **Hear Instructions.** Someone (boss, spouse, friend, child) asks you to do something or gives you some type of instructions.

2. **Reflect Back.** Use the reflection techniques you learned earlier to make sure you're clear about what is being asked.

3. **Create a Quick Plan.** Quickly, think about the final outcome and the first steps you will take to reach it.

4. **Ask Another Question.** Based on your quick plan, you've already unearthed some more questions. Ask them.

5. **Say "okay."** Now you may say "okay" and start the task.

6. **You might even add one little thing.** Use this opportunity to say to the requester, "As I begin this process, some questions may arise. If I have more questions may I come to you?" The answer, will, of course, be "yes." Now you have permission from two people to ask clarifying questions—the requester and *you*.

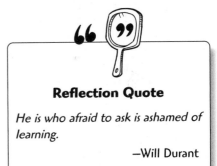

Reflection Quote

He is who afraid to ask is ashamed of learning.

—Will Durant

Why Don't You Ask Another Question?

The answer to this is not simple, but there are some common reasons:

➤ There isn't enough time to ask another question.

➤ You don't want to look stupid.

➤ You're not ready to face the task.

➤ You're overwhelmed at the thought of one more thing to do.

Unfortunately, these responses seem all too familiar. Well, let's look at the other side of this issue.

Why Must You Ask One More Question?

Once you reflect on what it is that keeps you from asking more probing questions, you are ready to think about this: asking questions is not just permissible, it's *necessary*. Why must you ask one more question?

➤ So that you can do the project/task right the first time

➤ To determine the latitude you have in accomplishing the task

➤ To clarify your understanding of the task

➤ So that you won't waste precious resources

Your first response to the expanded anatomy might be, "I can't afford to spend that time going through all those steps. I have to get this thing started."

Reflection Quote

We are all sculptors and painters, and our material is our own flesh and blood and bones.

—Henry David Thoreau

The fact is that you cannot afford not to spend the time. By investing the time in the expanded process, you save time and energy in the long run while at the same time delivering a better product.

When you follow the expanded "ask another question" technique, you will enjoy more life success. This success leads to higher self-esteem, which leads to confidence, which leads to stretching yourself, which leads to success, which leads to increased self-esteem…. You get the picture.

Keep Your Eyes on the Prize

You're probably sitting there thinking, "I know what ears have to do with listening, but what is this 'eye' stuff?" Actually, the eyes are incredible tools for listening. They serve a dual purpose. First, by providing eye contact, you demonstrate to the person talking that you are listening. Second, by using your eyes you can observe the relationship between the actions and words of the person talking. Let's look at these in a little more depth:

Action Prompt

Assume responsibility for your creatorship. It is one of those priceless gifts that can be used for everything from enjoying a peaceful moment to solving a complex problem.

1. By maintaining eye contact (not staring), you show that you are listening—you are present in the conversation. This is one of the most basic forms of *attending behavior*. You will find chapters devoted to attending behaviors in most general communication texts.

2. The second purpose is much more complex. Your eyes allow you to observe the nonverbal cues of the person talking. This enables you to determine the relationship between the actions and the words.

The question you must ask yourself is: "Self, are the actions and the words consistent?" For example, say your best friend says she's happy to see you and she is smiling, the words are consistent with the behavior. Once you have an answer you can climb the decision tree shown here.

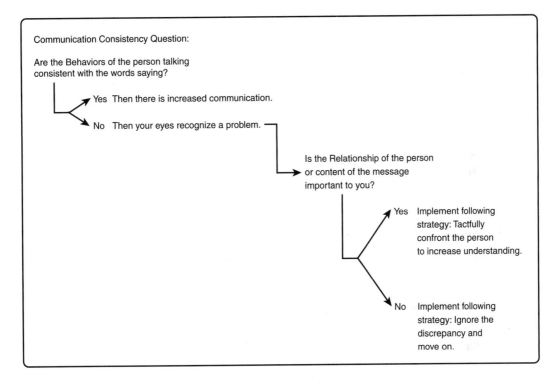

Communication Consistency Question:

Are the Behaviors of the person talking consistent with the words saying?

Yes Then there is increased communication.

No   Then your eyes recognize a problem.

Is the Relationship of the person or content of the message important to you?

Yes Implement following strategy: Tactfully confront the person to increase understanding.

No   Implement following strategy: Ignore the discrepancy and move on.

Decision tree.

So let's look at some possible scenarios.

If YES is the answer to the question, "Are the actions and the words of the person sending the message consistent?", then this is a no brainer. The behaviors emphasize the words and probably even strengthen the power of the message. Your understanding of the message is enhanced. Life is good.

However, if NO is the answer to the question, then this is where the fun begins. First of all you may thank your eyes: they've enabled you to pass the first test of sleuthing. You notice an inconsistency or discrepancy between the two modes of communication used by the person sending the message. This is where you have to work harder to decode the real message.

There are two sleuthing approaches you can use, depending on your commitment to the relationship between you and the other person and/or how important the content of the message itself is to you.

➤ If neither the relationship or the message being sent are of importance or great concern, you might just want to ignore the inconsistency and move on. For example, you are going through the check-out line at the grocery store and the cashier says, with a mean scowl on her face, "Thank you for shopping here, and have a nice day." This obviously is not worth your time and emotional investment.

➤ If the relationship and/or the message is important, it is essential to confront the person in a nonthreatening and tactful manner. Remember, confrontation does not have to be a negative endeavor. Unfortunately, our culture has tied negative strings to its meaning. You can positively address this issue. Say, for example, you're talking with a friend about renting an apartment together. You ask her if she wants to do it. With her legs and arms crossed, and a frown on her face, she replies in a stilted voice, "Sure, I'd love to." You cannot ignore this inconsistency. So what do you do?

Here is one sample response that might work. "You're saying "yes," but I'm sensing that you might have some misgivings or hesitancy about our renting an apartment together. Can we talk some more about it?"

Nice job! Now the issue is on the table. Nobody was threatened and a climate for understanding has been created. You can deal with the concerns, honor the relationship, and enhance the understanding. Of course, there are many responses you can use to open the dialogue—you just need to find out which fits you best. The benefit is understanding and openness.

Your eyes can be great communicators and detectives. Use them to their fullest potential.

Inspirational Injection

I'd Rather See a Sermon

I'd rather see a sermon than hear one any day.

I'd rather one should walk with me than merely show the way.

The eye's a better pupil, and more willing than the ear.

Fine counsel is confusing, but examples always clear.

I soon can learn to do it, if you'll let me see it done,

I can see your hands in action, but your tongue too fast may run.

And the lectures you deliver may be very fine and true,

But I'd rather get my lesson by observing what you do.

For I may misunderstand you and the high advice you give,

But there is no misunderstanding how you act and how you live.

—Unknown

Other Attending Behavior Hints

Of course, as any communications textbook will tell you, there are many other ways to show that you are paying attention to the other person when he or she is talking. Here are some of the most important.

➤ Use a subtle head nod to show the person you're with them—listening. I emphasize *subtle*. Don't be like the ceramic dog you got in grade school that has a spring for a neck, which causes it to violently shake up and down. That's distracting.

➤ Occasionally say "uh-huh," or "yes," or "I understand," or some other minimal utterance.

➤ Smile when appropriate, look concerned when appropriate. It is as important for your facial expressions to match the message the other person sends, as it is for your words to be consistent.

➤ Lean a little closer to the person talking. Close enough to show interest, but not too close—don't invade his or her personal space.

The key to all of these is moderation and subtlety.

Listening To Do List

To Do lists—are they a sign of the times or what?! They seem to have become part of our culture. So let's get started on a list. I'll give you some items, and you can create the rest:

➤ Carve out undivided time to spend with those folks close to you (friend, spouse, child).

➤ Minimize distractions when communicating. Go for a walk and talk. Get away from phone and faxes. Ask your secretary not to interrupt you.

➤ Make a commitment to communicate more effectively.

➤ _____

➤ _____

➤ _____

The Least You Need to Know

➤ Listening takes work—challenge yourself.

➤ Focus—in your own way.

➤ Elevate conversations to a personal level.

➤ Ask one more question—for the growth of it.

Chapter 21

To Touch or Not to Touch? That Is the Question

In This Chapter

➤ The essence of touch starts with *T*

➤ The "appropriate touch" factor

➤ Discover your daily dose requirements

➤ Touches a day keep the doctor away

Touch pad. Touch screen. Touch tone. Touch sensitive. What ever happened to "touch people"?

Think about what you have done today. Did you use the telephone? Did you use a fax machine? Did you use e-mail? Unfortunately, many of our conveniences have disrupted some of our other connections in life, like:

➤ Being face to face

➤ Seeing the feeling behind the words

➤ Hearing the emotions from deep within the heart

➤ Receiving a supportive touch

Our advanced technological living has removed us a step further away from people—and from touch. The person-to-person touch issue is a hard one to get your arms around. (Sorry, I couldn't resist.)

Take the "T" Out of Touch and You Are Left with "Ouch"

ABCDEFGHIJKLMNOPQRSUVWXYZ. The alphabet. You *are* quick. Remember the little blocks you used to play with as a child? You know, the wooden blocks that had one letter on each side, painted in primary colors. And then there was *the song*. I bet you can still sing the alphabet song today. Let's sing it together: ABCDEFG (big breath) HIJKLMNOP (big breath). OK. That's enough.

Actually, the alphabet you learned was different from the one that introduced this section. What's wrong with the one shown at the start of the last paragraph?

You're right. The *T* is missing, and *T* is the first letter of the word *touch*—and an extremely important letter, I might add. You see, if you take the *T* out of touch, you're left with *ouch*. That would be a painful state of affairs. The *T* stands for *therapeutic*. Tactile. Tenderness. The essential attributes of touch would be missing, and you in turn would be missing a lot.

Not only do you need to put the *T* back in touch, but you ought to make it a capital *T*.

Touch As Healer

Remember when you were a child and you fell off of your bike and scraped your knee? Do you recall what you did? Yes—you ran to your Mom for a big hug. Remember when a relative died and someone gave you comfort by holding your hand or putting their arms around you? These examples demonstrate the healing power of touch. When you scraped your knee and ran to your mother, you didn't say, "Whoa, Mom, don't touch me." Human beings depend on touch for healing.

Study after study demonstrates the power of touch in the healing process. The empirical data is great for those who need proof, but the reality is that you've probably already experienced first hand the healing power of touch in your life.

I used to take my two girls to a nursing home regularly to visit an elderly friend of ours. I was always amazed to see what happened when we walked down the hallways to our friend's room. Resident after resident would reach out to touch us—hoping for a handshake, a hug, or whatever human contact they could make, no matter how minimal. The power of touch, the need for touch, the hope for touch—all are profound aspects of the human condition.

You see the phenomenon of touch desire all the time with celebrities. Think of what happens when a famous actor or politician (could be the same person) goes out in public. Throngs of people wedge themselves into strategic positions to catch at least a glimpse, but really wanting to touch, the celebrity.

Untouchable? *Not*

There was a time in the history of the world when certain people were labeled as untouchable. Some folks would argue that this condition has been true during every era and is so even today. Not only is this disturbing, it is *wrong*. This type of mind-set erodes our society and undermines our sense of community. Atrocious, isn't it?

But another related issue is equally troubling. It's when an individual labels her- or himself as untouchable. If you don't pay attention to anything else in this book, please pay attention to this. *No one is untouchable.* Not you, not me—no one. Everyone has gifts, something to offer the world. One of life's challenges is to discover those gifts. You have a lot to offer. Acknowledge your talents, validate your personhood, and do not undermine yourself. Give yourself the healing and strengthening power of touch.

Let's think about that word, "heal." I'll save you time by looking up the word for you. Webster's says in its first definition that "heal" means "to make whole." That's a pretty powerful concept.

Action Prompt

Go to a nursing home and share an ear and a warm hand.

Human beings continually seek wholeness. But merely seeking is not enough. If you're going to truly heal yourself, then you have to be the change agent: you have to take action (sitting on the couch flipping through inspirational channels on TV is not enough). Trying a new behavior means you will have to try something new—novel concept, isn't it?

It's time for a pulse check. Pick up a #2 pencil (it doesn't really *have* to be a #2, I just like the sound of that), and answer the following:

Action Prompt

Treat Yourself to a Massage. Make the appointment today!

1. Where is a safe environment in which I can try a new touch behavior?

   _____

   _____

2. What appropriate touch behavior do I want to try?

   _____

   _____

3. After I experiment with the behavior, what questions should I ask myself to assess its impact?

   _____

   _____

4. What are the answers to the questions in number 3?

   _____

   _____

5. Should I try this behavior again? If yes, when and where? If no, what is another behavior I can try?

   _____

   _____

Appropriate Touch: A Touchy Issue

Imagine this scenario. You are a male (for some of you that will be harder to imagine than for others). You're interviewing secretarial candidates. The candidate sitting directly in front of you happens to be a female. She is very qualified. During the interview, you ask her the following question: "When you do a job well, what kind of recognition do you like?" She looks you straight in the eye and responds, "All I need is a pat on the back—as long as it is high enough."

Unconventional Wisdom

Why are some of us more willing to hug trees than to hug people?

Yes—the ol' appropriate touch issue raises its head, and appropriately so. We have already acknowledged the importance of touch in our lives, but touching cannot be done in random, indiscriminate, and unthoughtful ways. When you touch another person you must consider that person's needs, desires, and feelings. Not just your own.

Unfortunately, this touch issue is much more complex than it appears at first glance. What I may be very comfortable with, you may not. Bear hugs may be great for bears, but try giving a bear hug to a porcupine.

Think back to the way you were raised and what you were taught regarding the touch issue. You definitely created some preferences regarding touch in your life. A friend of mine comes from a big family where hugging is the norm. Once you step over the threshold of the front door, you become one of the hugged. Another friend of mine lives in a household where no hugging takes place among family members.

Action Prompt

The impact of touch in your life deeply affects your personhood, both positively and negatively. What is one thing you can do to make touch a more positive aspect of your life? Don't just think about this action, but recognize your worth and *do* it.

Assess Your Touch Situation

Use the following questions as a way to reflect on your own views about touch.

➤ What was the role of touch in your life, growing up?

_____

_____

➤ How did that impact the way you touch or view touch today?

_____

_____

➤ Are you content with the way you employ touch in your life, or do you want to modify it in some way? How would you change it?

_____

_____

➤ What is your definition of appropriate touch?

_____

_____

Get a Grip (So to Speak)

Appropriate touch is a complex issue. Although the components and appropriateness of human touch are multifaceted, convoluted, and highly unique to individuals—you have to get a grip! That's easy for *me* to say.

I feel strongly that our lives become much more manageable and enjoyable when we "destruct" the complexity and seek to simplify. So instead of a list of rules, I'll give you just one:

Unconventional Wisdom

Honor yourself by not letting someone else dishonor you.

The sublevel horizontal linear graphic representation is that Homo sapiens needs to provide unconditional regard for the tactile sensations we impress on the sensory receptors of other human life forms.

Oh, sorry. I did say simplicity was best, didn't I? OK, here is the rule in simple mode:

The bottom line is—respect yourself and others regarding touch.

Respect Yourself

Building on one half of that rule, keep the following ideas in mind for respecting yourself.

➤ Don't let someone touch you inappropriately.

➤ If someone does, be firm, direct, and clear that you do not appreciate it.

➤ Be specific: state exactly what they did that you do not like.

➤ Don't feel guilty about confronting someone. It is your body, your feelings, and your spirit that are involved.

Power Plate

IRSPCTU

➤ If you feel uncomfortable about how to tell someone that you don't appreciate their inappropriate touch, ask others for advice on the best way to deal with it. You have many resources (gifted friends, colleagues, and professionals who can support you). Remember—asking for help can be a good, healthy endeavor. Give yourself permission to ask for help.

Respect Others

There are several things to keep in mind when respecting the boundaries of others, but most of them boil down to common sense and a willingness to honor the other person.

➤ Gauge a person's personal-space needs before touching that person.

➤ Put yourself in the other persons' shoes (unless of course they wear a size 4 or 16). Remember that their attitudes and feelings about touch may be very different than yours.

➤ Recognize and respect the cultural influences surrounding the touch issue.

➤ When in doubt, ask: "Let's shake hands?" "Can I have a hug?" "Give me five!"

➤ Err on the side of less touch. On the issue of touch, more is not always better. Initially, create comfort zones with small gestures. As trust builds, then you will be able to judge whether to create opportunities for additional touch.

➤ Model appropriate touch behavior for others.

Unconventional Wisdom

Why is it that in some countries the personal-space comfort zone is three inches, while in other cultures the comfort zone is measured in feet? Where is *your* comfort zone?

Are You Getting Your Daily Requirement?

This is a multiple-choice quiz question. What do all packaged food items sold in stores have in common?

A. They cost money.

B. They are put in the grocery cart that has the bad wheel.

C. The coupon for the item you want expired yesterday.

D. The big sale item did just that: sell big; there are no more on the shelf.

E. All of the items have labels that tell what percentage of daily intake you need for optimal living.

F. All of the above.

The answer is probably *F,* all of the above—at least that has been my experience. But let's look at answer *E.* Upon closer inspection of the label on the package, the actual words are: "percent daily value." Great concept! But something is missing. You don't see anything showing the percentage of values needed for touch activities.

Just think—what if you were given a can of touch with this label on the back:

YES!

Power Plate

TCHALIF

Optimal Living Touch Facts

Touch Types	% Daily Value**
3 hugs	34%
2 kisses	21%
6 handshakes	18%
2 pats on the back	27%
Total	100%

** *percent daily values are based on your unique needs—which you determine.*

Now for the good news! There are no national standards for the amount of daily touch an individual needs. It's a personal thing—and that's the way it should be. The onus is on you to discover what your needs are. Take a moment and answer the following:

1. What kind of touch comforts me? (Examples: holding a hand, pat on the back, hug)

   _____

   _____

2. What kind of touch behaviors do I initiate to connect with others? (Example: Extend hand for handshake.)

   _____

   _____

3. What type of touch behaviors do I ask for? (Example: "Will you give me a hug? I need one!")

   _____

   _____

4. I have a good balance of touch in my life.   Yes   or   No   (Circle one.)

Based on the information in this list, create one, I repeat, *one* touch goal (a touch goal is different from a touchdown). Make the goal realistic, achievable, and measurable.

1. Goal: _____

   _____

   _____

2. Objectives: (Specific actions I will take to reach the goal)

_____

_____

3. Celebration Reward: (Identify what you will do to celebrate accomplishing your goal.)

_____

_____

Accept the challenge to strengthen the power of touch in your life. Ask for what you need, and then give yourself a pat on the back for making progress toward personal growth.

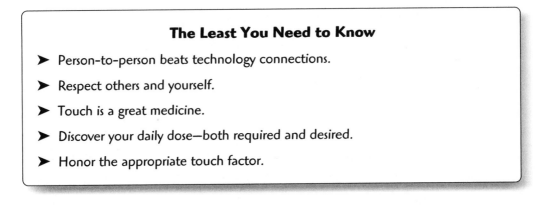

The Least You Need to Know

➤ Person-to-person beats technology connections.

➤ Respect others and yourself.

➤ Touch is a great medicine.

➤ Discover your daily dose—both required and desired.

➤ Honor the appropriate touch factor.

Part 8
Teamwork:
The Power of One Plus

There is no limit to what you can accomplish if you don't care who gets the credit.

Unknown

When we focus exclusively on what we want to accomplish on our own, we overlook the power of teamwork. There are no magic rules for making a team function effectively, but there are signs to watch for—why some teams fail and others succeed. As you work through this part of the book, you'll learn that self and others do not conflict: the pinnacle of self-esteem is also where you learn best how to work with others in a collaborative way.

Chapter 22

Successful Teams Don't Have to Have Superstars

In This Chapter

➤ What is this collaboration business?

➤ Vulnerability: strength or weakness?

➤ Why do teams fail?

➤ Why do teams succeed?

I heard a story recently about a mule pull in the '80s. (I'm not sure whether it was the 1980s or the 1880s. So what's a century?) Each mule was harnessed to a sled loaded with weights. The winning mule accomplished an incredible feat by pulling over 8,000 pounds. The second-place finisher pulled just shy of 8,000 pounds. The strength of these animals was truly amazing. After the official competition was over a bystander yelled out, "I wonder how much they could pull if they worked together?" Intrigued by the question, the mule owners attached one sled to the mules for a joint pull. To the astonishment of the onlookers, the pair of mules working together pulled over 30,000 pounds.

That is the power of collaboration. Whether mule or human, when you combine your gifts you are able to achieve much greater results than you can individually.

The Champion Question

Tennis champion. Track champion. Skateboard champion. Marathon champion. They seem to be individual achievers. But is that really the case? *No.*

Hmm. Certainly you've witnessed individuals accomplish great things. However, an individual did not become successful by her- or himself. Even in the solitary sports helpers were essential for the success—helpers called coaches, parents, teachers, and friends. No one can claim success as strictly his or her own.

This concept is true on the playing field, in the board room, in the classroom, and at home. It is the efforts of many that create successful lives.

The Vulnerability Factor

The key to success is vulnerability. Vulnerability is a strength. You might be thinking that we are wading in oxymoron waters again. We are. So put on your boots and let's get walking.

The only way to learn is to let yourself be vulnerable—to open yourself to learning. That means you have to admit to yourself:

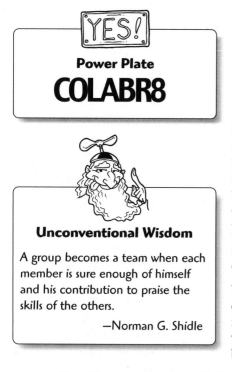

Power Plate

COLABR8

Unconventional Wisdom

A group becomes a team when each member is sure enough of himself and his contribution to praise the skills of the others.

—Norman G. Shidle

➤ I'm not perfect.

➤ I don't know it all.

➤ I'm not too old to learn something new.

➤ I do have the smarts to learn something new.

➤ It's not a weakness to ask for help.

Now, it's not a matter of just acquiescing to vulnerability. It is the marriage of vulnerability to a commitment to growth. Vulnerability becomes a tool for growth—one that allows you to experience life in new and exciting ways. Vulnerability is allowing yourself to team up with one or many other people to create a different you...and them.

Let's examine the nature of vulnerability a little more closely.

You can't always show your vulnerable self, just as you can't always be firm or strong. Mark Usry and I collaborated to create a continuum for examining the nature of vulnerability and a framework for its use. (See? I do believe in collaboration.)

Consider a continuum with four points: weak, vulnerable, strong, and unyielding. Now place a fulcrum between vulnerable and strong. As long as you move between these two points you will strike a healthy balance. If you spend all your time at the points weak and unyielding, however, there will be no balance or effectiveness. There are times when you need to be vulnerable and times when you need to be strong. Although this seems a paradox, the arrangement actually creates a wholeness that yields trust and fosters mutual success.

Inspirational Injection

I cannot promise you a lifetime or even a day

What I can offer is simply me

For whatever amount of time we can steal

I offer you laughter for laughter is beauty

I offer you honesty for honesty is pure

I offer you patience for patience is needed to gain trust

I offer you sincerity for through my sincerity

I will show you my inner being and desires

All I ask in return is for you to be honest and open,

For through your honesty and openness

I will receive from you all that I offer.

—Roger C. VanHorn

Our society constantly conveys messages to repress the vulnerable self: "Don't let them see you sweat," "You've got to be tough," "Cover up those mistakes." Certainly you have to show strength, but your successful relationships will be grounded and holistic—not one-dimensional.

By creating a holistic self you unleash your personal power, which you know has greater influence than position power. When your personal power is articulated through influence, persuasion, and shared purposes, you foster trust-oriented relationships that yield greater long- and short-term rewards.

Power Plate

GR8TEAM

Conduct a Personal S.W.O.T. Analysis

You can assess your vulnerability by conducting a personal S.W.O.T. analysis: examining your strengths, weaknesses, opportunities, and threats. You might find this difficult initially because your defense mechanisms may want to make their presence known. To combat the interference of your natural defenses, put on your armor of objectivity and answer the following:

1. What are your strengths?

    _____

    _____

2. What are your weaknesses?

    _____

    _____

3. What are your life opportunities?

    _____

    _____

4. What are your life threats?

    _____

    _____

The business world has used S.W.O.T. analyses for years. Now it's your chance to do so.

Benefits of Conducting a Personal S.W.O.T. Analysis

As you perform a S.W.O.T. analysis, there are many benefits you'll reap. Here are a few.

➤ You can create personal development plans.

➤ You can more effectively establish life and career plans.

➤ You can surround yourself with people of expertise to fill in the gaps.

➤ You can understand your life's "big picture."

Teams: the Good, the Bad, and the Effective

Everywhere you look, you see one of your friends or colleagues wearing a shirt or hat with their corporate logo snuggling up to the term "team." You might even own one of these pronouncement garments yourself. Teams, teams, everywhere teams.

Self-directed teams, research teams, marketing teams, volunteer teams, sports teams, disaster relief teams, and on and on and on.

You may be tired of the term, but the fact remains that individual and corporate success are the result of teamwork. Call it by another name if you want, but this is still the essence of success. A team can be made of 2 people or 2,002 people. (I know that one of you reading this is saying, "Well, how about 2003 people?"). Although teams contribute to successes, the fact remains that they don't always work. Why? Great question!

Reflection Quote

None of us is as smart as all of us.

—Unknown

Why Teams Fail

Teams fail for a variety of reasons:

➤ The wrong types of teams are used. There are many types of teams. One type of team is not the best tool for all types of situations. You need to choose the right type.

➤ People are afraid they'll lose control with the implementation of teams. Some folks create interdependent teams and then attempt to control them. This control paralyzes the teams, negatively impacts morale, and diminishes trust.

➤ There is a lack of clarity of what constitutes a team. Training and clarification are essential for a team to be successful.

➤ There is a lack of respect for group members' differences. Too often when we partner with others we act as though our fellow members are or should be just like us. When that happens, the real benefits of teamwork are diminished and opportunities for true growth are stifled.

Unconventional Wisdom

I may have to do something by myself, but I never have to do it alone.

John Hall, quoting one of his team-building participants

Unconventional Wisdom

Successful teams don't just happen—they are made!

How Teams Succeed

On the other hand, there are steps you can take to help your team be more successful:

➤ Demonstrate your respect for others. When you show respect for others your actions translate into maximizing the potential of

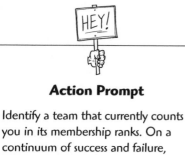

Action Prompt

Identify a team that currently counts you in its membership ranks. On a continuum of success and failure, where does this team fit? Write down two actions you can take to move it closer to the successful side of the continuum. Now employ the actions!

others. You create an environment in which gifts are freely shared and true synergy is fostered.

➤ Share goals. The most effective teams create shared goals. Think about yourself. When you work with someone else to achieve a common goal, you are much more likely to achieve success.

➤ Minimize outside influences that interfere with team performance. Team success happens when the processes, rules, goals, and actions are the domain of the team—not of external authorities. The more the team can "own itself," the more effective it will be.

Teams are a staple of success in our society. Creating them requires patience, respect, and commitment. May the team be with you!

Team Reflections

Take a minute to walk through the following reflection.

1. Reflect upon the most successful team of which you were a member. What are three characteristics that made it successful?

    a. _____

    b. _____

    c. _____

2. Reflect upon the least successful team of which you were a member. What are three characteristics that made it a failure?

    a. _____

    b. _____

    c. _____

In which team was membership more enjoyable? This is really a free answer because the answer is so simple. The successful team, of course. If your answer wasn't this, then we probably need to talk.

Brainstorm Team Slogans

Now is your time to get a bit creative. As we mentioned earlier, *teamitis* has hit the country. What are some slogans you have heard, seen on bumper stickers, viewed on baseball caps?

I'll get you started:

Say We not Me

T.E.A.M.—Together Each Achieves More

United we stand, divided we fall

_____

_____

_____

_____

_____

_____

Nice job. Teams are part of our culture, have always been part of our culture, and always will be. The more quickly we learn to appreciate and value them, the more successful we will be.

The Least You Need to Know

➤ Collaboration is essential for individual and team success.

➤ Vulnerability can be a great strength.

➤ Teams take time, commitment, and skill to succeed.

➤ Teams succeed when "we" replaces "me."

Chapter 23

The Teamwork-Soulwork Connection

In This Chapter

➤ What's your real business?

➤ Are you reaching far enough?

➤ How can you scale the empower tower?

➤ How are you able to enjoy the recapture rapture?

I like the word *reciprocity* because it deals with the notion of give and take. For families, communities, and societies to be successful, reciprocity has to be a hallmark of the system. The bottom line is that you benefit from the group's contributions and the group benefits from your contributions.

The more you develop your gifts, the more you have to offer others and the greater impact you can make on the world. So you have a dual commitment—to yourself and to your community. By growing each, you find that life flourishes in ways unexpected. These experiences add lustre.

Life Business Card

Business cards. They are everywhere. Don't get caught without one. We have a curious ritual in our society. I call it the "great business card exchange." Think about meetings you have attended that involved people from outside your organization. At some point in the meeting—of course, when the time is just right—someone says, "Here is my business card." Then the ritual begins. Everyone in the meeting pulls a little card from a gold or leather case (a case designed to impress) or from a pocketbook or wallet. These cards hold such information as a job title, name, phone number, fax number, e-mail address—the essentials. The cards are then exchanged.

The interesting thing about business cards is that they serve the person giving the card as much as the recipient. The business card tells us who we are—president, vice president, account manager, teacher, dentist. Think about the first job you got that required you to get a business card. If you're like most of us, you couldn't wait to get it printed so that you could see your name huddled next to this new title. A lot of emotional stock is invested in the words printed on these cards. The traditional business card only highlights a fraction of our personhood, however.

I recommend that you carry another type of business card with you. In fact I would be so bold as to say that it will be the most important card you can carry. Its title is "Life Business". It may look like a traditional business card, but rather than sharing a blip on your life screen, it shares a prescription for fulfilled living.

Don't limit yourself by what is on your traditional business card. Instead, stretch your potential by reaching toward the challenges that currently exceed your grasp. Where your traditional business card is about what is, Life Business is about future opportunities, gifts of growth, and the life you create. Here is the card I use—it also serves as a good summary of the main points I've discussed in these chapters. You'll find copies of it for your own use in the reference card at the front of this book.

"Life" Business Card

- Serve others unselfishly
- Respect yourself, children, the elderly, mother earth, your neighbors, and your colleagues
- Love others unconditionally
- Approach the day with the attitude: "I make a difference"
- Embrace the "choice factor"—the choices in life are yours and yours alone
- Laugh
- Make someone else's life brighter each day
- Listen, listen, listen

- Abandon mediocrity and strive for excellence
- Dream
- Establish daily, monthly, yearly, and life goals
- Cultivate your gifts, talents, and abilities
- Balance your life: integrate body, mind, spirit, and community
- Commit yourself to physical and nutritional well-being
- Slow Down, seek wonder, and live each moment

"You Make a Difference"

Inspirational Injection

Reaching Beyond

Do you reach beyond to touch the sky,
or lag behind, afraid to try?
Do you reach beyond to learn anew,
or hesitate—the same old you?
Do you reach beyond to test your limit,
or do you tell yourself, I'm timid?
Do you reach beyond to lead the pack,
or do you waste time looking back?
Do you reach beyond and strive to find
better ways to stretch your mind?
Do you reach beyond to care and share
and help some others do and dare?
Do you reach beyond, expect the best
or have you given up the quest?
Do you reach beyond and claim your space,
here and now, this time and place?
Do you reach beyond and try to soar,
or sadly, play it safe once more?

—Suzy Sutton

Empower State Building

Hmm. That's an odd title. Must be an odd author. Oh well. That's okay, because this empower state building is important business.

What does *empowerment* mean to you? To most of us, it is a vague notion caught in the new business vernacular trap.

Power Plate

LUVNLIF

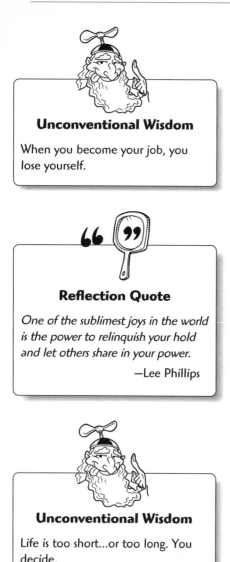

The term actually has a lot of merit, but in order to appreciate its power (sorry, I couldn't resist), let's make it operational it. Actually, I'm going to refer to one of my favorite definitions offered by philosopher and leadership writer, Peter Koestenbaum. He defines empowerment by using a mathematical formula. It follows:

$$E = D \times A \times S$$

where E = empowerment, D = direction, A = autonomy, and S = support.

Before I explain the formula further, I must apologize to philosopher Koestenbaum and add another piece to the formula:

$$E = D \times A \times S \times (T + A)$$

T = trust and A = accountability.

Okay. Are you ready for the math? The reason for the multiplication in this formula is that if any of the factors is a "0" then empowerment is "0." You won't have it. For empowerment to occur you have to have *direction*—you need to know where you are headed. You have to have *autonomy*—the freedom to do the job. You have to have *support*—the resources and emotional encouragement. And finally, you have to have *trust* and *accountability*. If trust is missing, so is empowerment. Accountability is essential for success.

When Koestenbaum created the original formula, he had in mind organizations and the teaching of leadership. This formula works equally well for personal empowerment. Personal empowerment is the highest level of empowerment. If you first empower yourself, you become a much better empowerer of others.

1. What is one thing you can do to empower yourself?

   _____

   _____

2. What action would you need to take to do it?

   _____

   _____

3. When would you be able to accomplish this action?

_____

_____

4. How would you measure your accomplishment of the action?

_____

_____

5. Who could help you succeed in taking this step?

_____

_____

Now you have all of the ingredients, why don't you get started?

Escape Is an Illusion

Houdini was a master of illusion. He freed himself from chains, locked trunks, and water death traps. He escaped what appeared to be life-threatening events.

Have you ever tried to be a Houdini escaping life's struggles? My guess is that your methods of escape might have been different from Houdini's.

➤ "I just need one more drink."

➤ "These drugs sure help numb my head."

➤ "I'm moving. I've got to get out of this town."

Changing landscapes or modifying physiological ones might create masks of escape, but they are just that—masks. The reality is that there *is* no escape, because we are always with ourselves. If I move, I'm still with me. If I have another drink, I'm still with me. If I do more drugs, I'm still with me.

There is no true escape and, contrary to what you might be thinking, that is the *good* news. The challenge of life is to experience and grow, not to escape. If you spend your life numbing or avoiding, you will miss out on the tremendous opportunities for transforming your life into one of fulfillment. Escape is living from the past and limiting the future. Fulfilled living is learning from the past and creating an exhilarating future.

Throughout this entire book I have talked about choice. The choice of creating a fantastic future is up to you. *Choose it!*

Today Is the Day

Today is the day...to live and to love it! If you wait until tomorrow you'll never have a fulfilled life. I guarantee it. Tomorrow's vision and yesterday's memory are nothing without today. A fully lived today creates cherished memories of yesteryear and high hopes for future dreams. Today is the day you can have an impact on your life and the lives of others. You can step beyond the secure footholds of mediocrity and scale the mountains of achievement. You are the only one who can advance yourself and soar to new heights. You have gifts, talents, and abilities to make yourself a wonderful success.

Enjoy the journey.

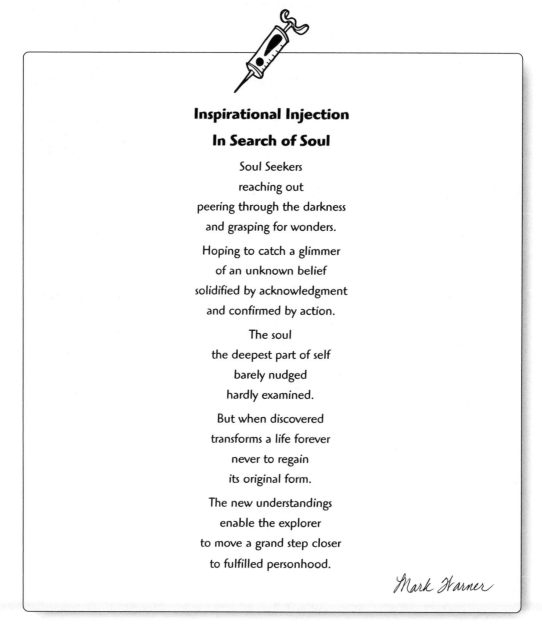

Inspirational Injection

In Search of Soul

Soul Seekers
reaching out
peering through the darkness
and grasping for wonders.

Hoping to catch a glimmer
of an unknown belief
solidified by acknowledgment
and confirmed by action.

The soul
the deepest part of self
barely nudged
hardly examined.

But when discovered
transforms a life forever
never to regain
its original form.

The new understandings
enable the explorer
to move a grand step closer
to fulfilled personhood.

Mark Warner

Recapture Your Life

Do you ever feel chained by the expectations of others? Do you ever feel pressured to conform to societal shoulds? Do you ever feel cramped by human-made rules and conditions? Do you ever feel exhausted by unrealistic personal expectations?

Too often the lines between reality and nonreality get blurred. Our vision gets tainted by the external voices that permeate our lives. Unfortunately, we move aside our own thoughts, feelings, and beliefs erroneously thinking that the external voices are right.

It's time to recapture your life. Take control of your existence. Listen to the voices within. Acknowledge your true feelings and beliefs. Accept life as it is. Listen to yourself, for on this earth you are the greatest authority of your being. You determine your destination.

Power Plate

2DAYZIT

Certainly you are interdependent and you must rely on others to succeed. Reliance on others does not mean relinquishing control of your personhood, however.

You have been blessed as no other person in the world has. Your uniqueness is what allows you to make an indelible imprint on the lives of others.

Action Prompt

Leaf back through this book and try one of the Action Prompts you skipped. Changing your life is an active, not passive, process.

Perpetuate your uniqueness. Get in the cycle of enhancing your particular gifts. By affirming and living these gifts, you strengthen them and foster others. This cycle allows you to break out of the "I'll be like others expect me to be" mode. You will find an increased zest for life, heightened energy, a new way of seeing the world, and a refreshed sense of being.

Life is to be lived and loved. Embrace it.

Inspirational Injection

Normal Day

Normal Day, let me be aware of the treasure you are.

Let me learn from you, love you, savor you, bless you before you depart.

Let me not pass you by in quest of some rare and perfect tomorrow.

Let me hold you while I may, for it will not always be so.

One day I shall dig my fingers into the earth, or bury my face in the pillow or stretch myself taut, or raise my hands to the sky, and want more than all the world your return.

—Mary Jean Irion

The Least You Need to Know

➤ Life Business is your only business.

➤ The only landscape you can change is your mind.

➤ Make today count.

➤ By discovering what is unique about you, you can recapture your life.

242

Chapter 24

Success Unlimited

In This Chapter

➤ Inferiority. Who invited it?

➤ Is failure really necessary for success?

➤ Are you a spark or a bad apple?

➤ How can you become a "successory"?

The intruder comes, uninvited and ready for action. It has been known by many names, but *inferiority* is the most common. I say it comes uninvited, but that is not exactly correct. For the reality is that we open the door and let inferiority in. Sometimes consciously, but we usually let it in by default—we don't proactively keep it out.

I also stated that inferiority is ready for action. It may be ready for action, but it can't exist without being given power from us. We provide the fuel that gives energy and form to this nemesis.

Why would we ever do that?

Usually it's a subconscious thing. We've let ourselves be ruled by the negative voices of the past. We've let those voices control our thoughts, emotions, and behaviors. We've tricked ourselves into believing that we are not worthy.

Vanquish the Inferiority Intruder

The premise that one human being is inferior to another human being is false. No one is inferior to anyone else. Sure, we all have areas in our lives where we are not as good as others, and other areas where we are better than others. But just because I can't do something as well as someone else does not make me an inferior person.

We must acknowledge our talents, not invite inferiority into our lives—and certainly not fuel its fury. We are solely in charge of the creature called inferiority. The job as head vanquisher is ours.

The Failure Advantage

Hear ye! Hear ye! The difference between successful and unsuccessful people is what they do with their failures.

What do you do with failed attempts?

➤ Do you let them demoralize you?

➤ Do you allow them to be a sword that pierces your self-esteem?

➤ Do you permit them to be another excuse so that you won't have to face success?

➤ Do you let them paralyze you?

Successful folks use failure as a springboard to greatness. From inventions to sonnets, from biotechnological research to painting abstracts, from crafting words to creating a bridge, from practicing law to practicing a golf swing—those who are successful know that failed attempts are a necessary ingredient for success.

Successful people understand that when you try something new, you can't jump from step 1 to step 5 and skip the intermediate steps. When we try that type of jump and are not successful, we say we can't do it and give up. But we must try a different approach and allow the failure to be the stepping stone that leads to achievement. Don't set yourself up for disappointment. Recognize that failures accompany success.

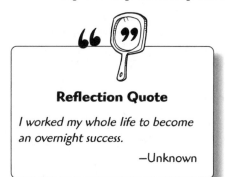

Reflection Quote

I worked my whole life to become an overnight success.

—Unknown

Of course you will experience failure at first. But don't get trapped into comparing an initial attempt with a final goal. Rather, compare each attempt with previous accomplishments. Most of the time you have exceeded past efforts. Don't devalue the small successes along the way, because they become the foundation for growth.

Begetter Cycle

What? A "begetter cycle"? It goes something like this: self-esteem begets success and success begets self-esteem and self-esteem begets success....

This is the original chicken-and-egg dilemma. Which came first? Actually this is the great cycle of growth. Jump in anytime you want. You decide when you truly want to be successful. However, one key to success is to set realistic goals and standards of achievement so that you can experience success. And when you've experienced some success, you'll feel better about yourself, because you have garnered some confidence and are ready for the next challenge level. The cycle continues.

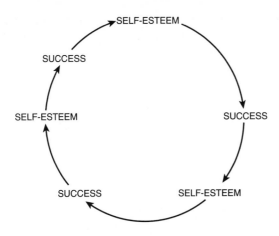

Don't forget that the successes are made up of many failed attempts, so you have to give yourself permission to learn from them and use them to get to your success. The mere acknowledgment that failure is a natural part of the process prevents paralysis and negativity, thus promoting positive steps towards growth.

The Price of Success

I attended a banquet honoring a benefactor of our university who happened to be the CEO of a major poultry company. During his talk, he stated, "You can get to the top of an organization in one of two ways: (1) work diligently and intelligently, or (2) inherit the business your Daddy started. I chose the latter." Most of us, however, have to earn it.

There is a price for success, and it takes many forms:

➤ Commitment

➤ Dedication

➤ Passion

➤ Preparation

➤ Desire

➤ Hard work

➤ Smart efforts

Unconventional Wisdom

Success is not free of charge.

Unconventional Wisdom

Try not to become a success, but rather try to become a person of value.

—Albert Einstein

Passive submission to challenges will not yield success. You have to be willing to pay the price—to stretch yourself and to work through, past, and around obstacles. But most of all you must believe in what you are doing. When you combine all these components, nothing is beyond your grasp. There are no limits.

Dynamic Changes

Just as you can exceed your own expectations as an individual, when you are involved with others in an endeavor the collaborative efforts can help you excel also. The subtitle of this section could be "the dynamics of 1." When it comes to teams, one person changes the entire team. The individual can be the spark that ignites enthusiasm or the bad apple that stinks up the place. Regardless of the type of contribution, the team dynamics change with the addition or deletion of one individual. So—are you the spark or the bad apple?

➤ **Definition of a spark:** Keeps things lit. On the move. Contributes. Energizes.

➤ **Definition of a bad apple:** Distracts. Passive. Disrupts. Impedes progress. Saps energy.

My guess is that your place on the apple/spark continuum changes depending on the organization you work for.

What makes you a bad apple? When you:

➤ Don't really want to be a member of the team.

➤ Don't like the way things are being done.

➤ Are not allowed to contribute the way you would like.

➤ Are not passionate about the team goals.

➤ Haven't bonded with others in the group.

➤ Haven't been able to get fully involved with the team.

➤ Just like bein' contrary (as my Grandmother used to say).

Power Plate

URUN–LTD

Reflection Quote

Success seems to be connected with action. Successful people keep moving. They make mistakes but they don't quit.

—Conrad Hilton

So how do you escape the bad apple experience? Change your mindset. Increase the level and type of involvement. Or change the geography—leave the group.

What, then, makes you a spark? When you:

➤ Are passionate about the mission and goals of the team.

➤ Are very involved.

➤ Believe in what you are doing.

➤ Enjoy the other folks you are working with.

➤ Feel as though you are making a contribution.

There is a caveat that sparks need to heed. Too much sparkin' can cause you to burn out. Carefully choose the groups in which you want to invest your time and energy. You never have to be a bad apple, but you don't always have to be a spark.

So you see—one person changes a group.

Identify three groups you belong to. (Family counts as a group.) Then identify whether you are a spark, a bad apple, or somewhere else on the continuum. If you are a spark, pat yourself on the back. If you are a spark in too many groups, decide whether you should continue to be a spark. For those groups in which you are either a bad apple or at least not a great contributor, take action. Either set goals to enhance your participation level or get out! (The completion of this action will give you a chance to work on your integrity enhancement.)

Group 1_____

    Spark, bad apple, or other:

    _____

    Positive Action:

    _____

    _____

    _____

Group 2_____

    Spark, bad apple, or other:

    _____

    Positive Action:

    _____

    _____

    _____

Group 3_____

    Spark, bad apple, or other:

    _____

    Positive Action:

    _____

    _____

    _____

Bench Sitters and Starters

Every individual on every team plays an important role. Some are in the spotlight so much that they see stars. Others have adorned the bench so much that they look like permanent fixtures. The fact of the matter is that everyone has an essential role to play.

Reflection Quote

Be brave enough to accept the help of others.

—Melba Cosgrove

In college I played on the tennis team. Or maybe I should say that I was a *member* of the tennis team. I was one of the bench-fixture types. I was so low on the ladder that you would have had to dig a hole to find me. I stayed on the team, though, because I knew that I was making a contribution—maybe not through my tennis prowess, but through my attitude and involvement in other ways. My tennis colleagues also contributed to my life and sense of self.

We can't all be the stars, but we all can be supporters.

A Team for the Ages

The year was 1980. The site was Lake Placid. The occasion was the XIII Winter Olympiad. It was the epic story of David and Goliath, replayed during the modern era. The arena was an ice rink. The contestants wielded sticks to maneuver the rock-hard puck. The contemporary David was dressed in the garb of the USA. The giant wore a Soviet Union tunic. The Goliath of ice hockey was heavily favored to win, having won the previous four Winter Olympics gold medals.

The history of Olympic ice hockey was rewritten that day. It was not rewritten because of a superstar but rather because of the incredible spirit of "ordinary" people. The USA players invested their hearts, souls, and bodies in a concept called *team*. These extraordinary individuals touched the lives of many, demonstrated the immense power of teamwork, and defeated the Soviet Union Goliath.

This group of noble skaters was team personified. Their story was not created by Hollywood, and their achievements were not due to luck. Instead, their success was due to:

➤ Their belief in each other

➤ Their willingness to share their individual gifts

➤ Their lack of concern over who would get the credit

➤ Their myopic focus on team goals.

The example of the USA team provides great lessons that you can apply and, in turn, use to inspire others. You can be a great contributor as well.

Oh, by the way, did I mention that after the USA conquered the Soviet Union they went on to the gold medal round and beat Finland? Teamwork is the power.

That Could Never Be Me

We hear about these impressive sports figures and inventors and writers, and sometimes we think, "That could never be me." We tend to think that all the stars, all the giants, all the movers and shakers have to be "out there" somewhere in a different town, a different school, a different company. But that is simply not the case.

You can have that same kind of success. That can be you. Your own successes, however, will reflect who you are, and you may receive a different level of public acknowledgment, but you can enjoy the same personal satisfaction from attaining your goals.

The way to become that successful person comes back to:

➤ Living your passion

➤ Believing in yourself

➤ Creating actions to accomplish your goals

➤ Asking for help in attaining your goals

➤ Recognizing your own accomplishments (which happens to be much more important than any external recognition you might receive)

Power Plate

Be a Successory

You've heard of being an accessory? How about a *successory*—a person who contributes to another's success? One of the greatest gifts you can give to other people is to support them in reaching their goals. You can be a successory. There are myriad ways and opportunities to perform this important and caring role.

Whether for a family member, a friend, a colleague, or a teammate, you can be instrumental in helping that person become successful. Just by believing in the person, you provide an incredible wealth of support. When you go above and beyond this to help, your efforts take on immense power.

No one can become successful on his or her own. We know that to be a fact. Others need *you!*

The magic in all this is that there are really *two* successes: the other person and you. When you aid in another person's efforts, you both become successful. You also get the added benefit of enjoying their success vicariously. Some people in this ol' world actually find more joy in helping others succeed than they find in their own personal success.

Success: The Benefits Abound

There is only one key to success: *you!* By unlocking your potential and unleashing your talents, skills, and abilities you can reap many fantastic rewards. Contrary to what

Madison Avenue would like us to believe, the greatest rewards are intangible. Tangible rewards such as money, a house on the coast, a fancy title, or a sports car are secondary at best. The intangibles enhance our lives and change us forever.

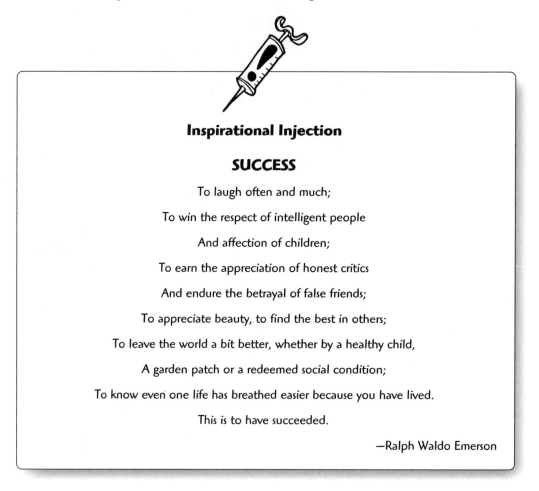

Inspirational Injection

SUCCESS

To laugh often and much;

To win the respect of intelligent people

And affection of children;

To earn the appreciation of honest critics

And endure the betrayal of false friends;

To appreciate beauty, to find the best in others;

To leave the world a bit better, whether by a healthy child,

A garden patch or a redeemed social condition;

To know even one life has breathed easier because you have lived.

This is to have succeeded.

—Ralph Waldo Emerson

The Least You Need to Know

➤ Uninvite inferiority; it is not a friend.

➤ One person has the power to change a whole team.

➤ Intangibles are the greatest rewards.

➤ Teams can work miracles.

➤ Be a successory.

Chapter 25

Final Thoughts

The last chapter. I've enjoyed our journey together. Since you've started this book, we are both different. It's true. You're not the same person nor am I. We've had some experiences, we've laughed, we've cried, we've learned, and most of all—we were the ultimate us. Before we part ways, however, I want to leave you with some concluding thoughts to reflect upon.

Review the Opening Letter

Turn to the opening letter in the book. This will be the third time you've read it. (You read it a second time as part of an activity in an earlier chapter.) As you reread the letter, think about the following questions dealing with "The Why or Why Nots":

➤ Was the book I thought I bought the book I read? Why or why not?

_____

_____

➤ Did the book deliver what it purported to deliver? Why or why not?

_____

_____

➤ Were the recommendations for reading the book helpful? Why or why not?

_____

_____

➤ Did the book really serve my purpose? Why or why not?

_____

_____

➤ What is the greatest thing I learned from the book?

_____

_____

Put the Book Aside

You're going to want to move the book from under your pillow or from its most recent home and put it aside for a while. I know that might cause some separation anxiety, but that too is part of growth.

You've taken some big steps during our journey and discovered many facets of your being in a short period of time. Now it's time for your subconscious and intuition to work their magic. Your body, mind, and spirit need the opportunity to massage the information, grasp its meaning, and digest the fruits. This is the second phase of learning.

Note: Put the book in a place, where it is easily retrievable.

Mark Your Calendar

You need to go and get your planner or calendar. Turn it to one year from today. Write in that spot: "Revisit the book." You'll know which one.

Challenge yourself to reread the book. You'll be intrigued to discover that it is a different book than the one you just completed. Yes, many of the principles will remain the same, but you bring different eyes with which to view the pages. You'll discover new riches, fresh insights, and new meanings behind many of the ideas and thoughts. Your literary companion will once again reveal secrets of fulfilled living. The book will be different because *you* will be different.

Well, you've made it to the end of the book. Thanks for sharing part of your life trek with me. Your future is bright and your adventures will be many. *Create a great life!*

The *Very* Least You Need to Know

➤ The luster of your life is up to you—no one else.

➤ You have some incredible gifts, talents, and abilities.

➤ You have the opportunity to make a profound difference in this world—do it.

➤ Touch someone else's life and yours too will be transformed.

➤ Live and love it!

Bibliography

Bach, R. *Illusions: the Adventures of a Reluctant Messiah.* (New York, Delacorte Press, 1977).

Bennis, W. G. *On Becoming a Leader.* (New York, Addison Wesley, 1989).

Blanchard, K. & Peale, N. V. *The Power of Ethical Management.* (New York, Wm. Morrow and Co., 1988).

Cooper, K. H. *The Aerobics Way.* (New York, Bantam Books, 1969).

_____. *The New Aerobics.* (Philadelphia, Lippincott, 1970).

Kopp, S. *If You Meet the Buddha on the Road, Kill Him!* (New York, Bantam Books, 1972).

Koestenbaum, P. *Leadership: the Inner Side of Greatness.* (San Francisco, Jossey-Bass Publishers, 1991).

Kouzes, J. M. & Posner, B. Z. *Credibility.* (San Francisco, Jossey-Bass Publishers, 1993).

Powell, J. *A Reason to Live! A Reason to Die!* (Niles, Ill., Argus Communications, 1975).

_____. *He Touched Me.* (Niles, Ill., Argus Communications).

Warner, M. J. "Enhancing Self-Esteem." *Executive Excellence: the Magazine of Leadership Development, Managerial Effectiveness, and Organizational Productivity* (11, no. 2, 1994).

_____. "Executive Vulnerability." *Executive Excellence: the Magazine of Leadership Development, Managerial Effectiveness, and Organizational Productivity* (14, no. 9, (1997).

_____. and Usry, M. L. "In Search of Soul." *Personal Excellence: the Magazine of Life Enrichment* (March, 1996).

_____. "Life Cards." *Personal Excellence: the Magazine of Life Enrichment* (1997).

_____. "Life Transitions." *Executive Excellence: the Magazine of Leadership Development, Managerial Effectiveness, and Organizational Productivity* (11, no. 5, 1994).

_____. "Why Teams Fail, How Teams Succeed." *Executive Excellence: the Magazine of Leadership Development, Managerial Effectiveness, and Organizational Productivity* (12, no. 6, 1995).

Index

M

Q

Check Out These
Best-Selling
COMPLETE IDIOT'S GUIDES®

Understanding **Catholicism**
SECOND EDITION
1-59257-085-2
$18.95

Learning Spanish
THIRD EDITION
0-02-864451-4
$18.95

The **Bible**
SECOND EDITION
0-02-864382-8
$18.95

Being a **Groom**
SECOND EDITION
0-02-864456-5
$9.95

Grammar and Style
SECOND EDITION
1-59257-115-8
$16.95

Playing the **Guitar**
SECOND EDITION
0-02-864244-9
$21.95 w/CD

Personal Finance in Your **20s & 30s**
SECOND EDITION
0-02-864374-7
$19.95

Knitting and Crocheting
SECOND EDITION *Illustrated*
1-59257-089-5
$16.95

The **Perfect Resume**
THIRD EDITION
0-02-864440-9
$14.95

Buying and Selling a Home
FOURTH EDITION
1-59257-120-4
$18.95

Low-Carb Meals
1-59257-180-8
$18.95

Calculus
0-02-864365-8
$18.95

More than *450 titles* in *30 different categories*
Available at booksellers everywhere

ALPHA